Population and Politics since 1750

William H. McNeill

Population

AND

Politics

SINCE

1750

UNIVERSITY PRESS OF VIRGINIA

Charlottesville and London

The Richard Lectures for 1988–89
UNIVERSITY   OF   VIRGINIA

THE UNIVERSITY PRESS OF VIRGINIA
Copyright © 1990 by the Rector and Visitors
of the University of Virginia

First published 1990

Library of Congress Cataloging-in-Publication Data
McNeill, William Hardy, 1917–
   Population and politics since 1750

   (The Richard lectures for 1988–89, University of
Virginia)
   Includes bibliographical references (p.   )
   1. Population—History.   2. Population—Political
aspects—History.   3. Europe—Population—History.
4. Europe—Population—Political aspects—History.
I. Title.   II. Series: Richard lectures ; 1988–89.
HB849.4.M4   1990   304.6'2   89-28772
ISBN 0-8139-1257-1

Printed in the United States of America

CONTENTS

PREFACE

The text of this little book is a slightly expanded version of the Richard lectures delivered at the University of Virginia on April 10, 12, and 14, 1989. I am grateful to the committee that invited me to give these lectures for the stimulus of having to find something to say. The further fact that the Woodrow Wilson Center for Scholars accorded me the privilege of residing in Washington and using the facilities of the Library of Congress for three months before the delivery of these lectures made their preparation possible. The informal contacts with other visiting scholars and with some of the leaders of American government that residence at the Woodrow Wilson Center involves were a pleasure in themselves and a real help in giving final form to my thoughts about the demographic diapason that, like the drones of the bagpipe, sets a background tone against which the shriller voices of political debate compete for attention.

Population and Politics since 1750

I

THE POLITICS OF
EXPANDING POPULATIONS:
EUROPE

Politics, being a distinctively human affair, is obviously rooted in the existence of human populations that in turn depend upon a perpetual and precarious balance between births and deaths for their continued existence. Reproduction, both biological and cultural, is not automatic or unchanging; and when any notable alteration in rates of growth and decay occur, the group concerned creates critical problems for itself and, often, for its neighbors as well. I propose to explore this level of human affairs as best I am able, with attention focused for the most part on the past 250 years.

The reason for choosing this horizon point is that about 1750 rates of population growth accelerated dramatically in some important parts of the civilized world, and rapid growth became global by 1850. In western Europe, where study of historical demography is much more advanced than elsewhere, experts have found that before the mid-eighteenth century periodic bad years when deaths far exceeded births very nearly balanced the normal excess of births that prevailed in years when disaster did not afflict the community. Short spurts of population growth were therefore quite usual, but so were sharp setbacks, reducing total numbers to or below the level at which growth had begun. A human life unaffected by famine, pestilence, and war was rare indeed, but, of course, the incidence and severity of demographic disaster varied from place to place as well as from time to time in confusing (though not quite random) fashion.

In the sixteenth and seventeenth centuries, as far as western Europe is concerned, the overall tilt of the resulting sawtooth pattern of population growth and decay was upwards, but only at a modest rate of .2 percent per annum. Moreover, this growth may be conceived as being the final lap of a long-drawn-out recovery from the enormous and exceptional disaster of the Black Death, which cut back European populations by about a third in a mere three years (1346–49). In western Europe as a whole, totals achieved by 1700 did not much surpass what had been attained in 1345 before the plague struck; and there were parts of Europe, e.g., in central Italy, where population totals were no higher than had prevailed in Roman times.

But older limits were soon left behind by what happened after 1750. Once pestilence and famine ceased to cut back local populations with their accustomed frequency and severity, sustained growth set in. By the beginning of the nineteenth century, annual rates of increase in different countries of Europe jumped to anything between .5 percent and 1.5 percent per annum, that is, to two and a half to seven times the rate that had prevailed in the centuries before. Total population of Europe therefore grew from about 118 million in 1700 to 187 million by 1801, and to 321 million by 1900. A similar spurt took place in China, where demographic data are also quite reliable. As a result, China's population more than doubled in the eighteenth century, rising from about 150 million to 313 million.

Elsewhere evidence is unsatisfactory, and in Japan, India, and the Middle East signs of sustained population growth like that of Europe and China do not become clear until after 1850. In the Americas, rapid growth of white and mestizo populations outweighed the continued decay of Amerindian populations in course of the eighteenth century, if not before; and black slave populations in North America

2

also began to grow by natural increase in the same period of time. As for Africa, no overall estimate is really possible. Intensified ravages of the slave trade in the eighteenth century did not prevent some populations from growing rapidly, although others, like the Khoikhoi and Pygmies, were suffering disruption and decay.[1]

Such widespread population growth was unprecedented, and its onset defines the modern era of demographic history in which we are still immersed. The only global transformation that can be compared to what happened between 1750 and 1850 was prehistoric, when village communities first began to cultivate the soil, allowing human numbers far to surpass older limits wherever agriculture spread.[2]

In the ten millennia (more or less) between these two demographic landmarks, despite innumerable local setbacks, human numbers tended to increase, and civilized societies expanded from small initial foci to occupy a substantial portion of the Eurasian continent. In the New World, Amerindian civilizations also expanded from their earliest centers, but the whole process lagged behind Eurasia by something like three thousand years and was abruptly cut off by the Spaniards after 1500. Critical development therefore centered in Eurasia, where eventually separate civilizations began to impinge on one another continuously so as to establish an ecumenical or Eurasian world system, held together by an accelerating exchange of goods, skills, ideas, and, not least, diseases. It is my belief that the new demographic regime that came to prevail between 1750 and 1850 reflected the impact of this Eurasian world system on human ecology.

In modern times, before medical science altered our exposure to infections, large and dense human populations sustained a class of childhood diseases—smallpox, measles, mumps, whooping cough, and others. These infections cannot survive among small, isolated human communities because they require a perpetual supply of newborns who have not yet acquired the lifelong immunities the disease provokes among survivors. These are, therefore, uniquely diseases of

3

civilization. Populations inured to them have a truly lethal epidemiological advantage whenever they enter into contact with disease-inexperienced peoples who lack civilized levels of resistance to such infections.

To begin with, these as well as other infections did not attain their full potential range across the face of the earth. As a result, one important side effect of the improvement of transport and intensification of trade and other contacts was to allow human diseases to attain whatever natural limits climate, population densities, and local modes of life established for them. This took a long time and involved serious setbacks to civilized populations whenever a new lethal infection first arrived in a particular part of the ecumene. The Black Death of the fourteenth century was the most important such event in medieval times. Other equally severe epidemic die-offs had occurred deeper in the past but were largely forgotten owing to defective records.

By the mid-eighteenth century, the network of transport and communication had reached such a point that in at least two important regions of the world—to wit, Europe and China—new disease exposures ceased to occur because hosts and parasites had established nearly stable relationships with one another. In these lands, infections were never absent from a given locality for long, and those viruses that provoked lifelong immunities among survivors therefore turned into childhood diseases.

It may seem paradoxical to suggest that peoples among whom exposure to serious and often lethal infections had become nearly universal would respond to disease saturation with the modern growth of population. But a moment's reflection will suggest that when diseases become endemic, epidemics lose nearly all their importance simply because most of the population is always immunized by an earlier encounter with the disease in question. Child mortality may be expected to increase under such circumstances; but even if that were the case (and for reasons not completely understood, children resist many infections better than young adults), it is

4

also true that an infant's loss could be replaced quickly and at small cost. Infant deaths did not endanger survival of other family members, as the death of the breadwinner might do. In fact, the death of a child might well provoke bereaved parents to try to replace it, and in any case, an infant's disappearance from the family would not delay or inhibit further births as a parental death was bound to do. Thus it is clear that when disease deaths concentrated among the very young, household disruptions arising from disease diminished drastically as compared to what had happened when sporadic exposure to epidemics put old and young equally at risk.[3]

It seems plausible to connect the modern surge of population growth with this changed incidence of exposure to lethal infections. The fact that China and Europe led the way fits the hypothesis very nicely, for China and Europe had far more capacious and finely reticulated systems of internal transport in early modern times than other lands.[4] In proportion as these transport systems united their respective populations into a single disease pool, the global homogenization of infections, established at principal ports of the earth by oceangoing ships after 1500, became capable of reaching inland so as to alter the disease experience of the whole society. Elsewhere the shift to endemicity took longer and was not completed before about 1850 when further improvements of transport affected all the inhabited earth, allowing the modern growth of population to become genuinely global.

Obviously, all sorts of circumstances, differing from place to place, affected the actual expression of the new demographic regime. Population growth could not continue very long without enlarged food supplies, for example; and contriving a distribution system capable of matching growing numbers with access to adequate food was never automatic.

Population growth therefore put strains on every society in which it manifested itself, and responses varied enormously. Such local variability, however, ought not to disguise the fact that the general volatility of modern times, which

5

distinguishes the last 250 years from earlier ages, was driven from below by population growth that simply does not allow the rural majority of humankind to hold fast to familiar customs and routines of work. Consequent departures from immemorial custom and village practices, now worldwide, mark off our age from all that have gone before. All humankind is affected. No matter how urbanized our own daily lives may have become, when the vast peasant (now ex-peasant) mass begins to move, the rest of us are borne along whether we wish it or not.

Rural life may never have been as stable and unchanging as city dwellers like to imagine. But as long as village births and deaths almost matched one another, one generation could follow another on the land, forming new households in accord with age-old family practices so as to maintain the village community as before—more or less. But when systematic population growth set in, rural society became a ticking time bomb. Sooner or later, the rising generation was sure to run out of local access to suitable land on which to pursue the even tenor of its ways. When that happened, behavior had to change, not just for an elite but for the majority—indeed for everybody. Human society is still staggering under this momentous departure from rural routines; and because the modern growth of population has by no means run its course, we must expect further upheavals, especially in view of the fact that some populations have stopped growing and will, if present trends continue, begin to shrink while others are still in full spate of growth. Such a juxtaposition of growing and shrinking populations creates a new context for human affairs. It seems worth reflecting on what the political consequences of growing and shrinking populations have been and are likely to be in time to come. Hence my choice of subject.

When land runs short in a rural community the most obvious thing to do is to try to maintain traditional ways of life by finding suitable land somewhere else and taking possession of it, if need be by force. When a community is au-

6

tonomous and cohesive and borders on other communities at a similar level of organization, that is indeed the prevailing response. The history of ancient times abounds in examples of how a people, impelled by population pressure on existing modes of life, attacked its neighbors and took their land away. The early history of such imperial polities as Athens and Rome illustrates this very clearly. So, in all probability, did Germanic encroachment on the Rhinelands and Britain in the fourth and fifth centuries and the Viking raids of the ninth and tenth. The massacre of Glencoe shows that Scottish clans were doing the same as recently as 1692. Innumerable other instances, some recorded, others not, constituted a very prominent feature of early human history.

It is worth noting that such direct, straightforward responses to land hunger always turned out to be self-limiting. Successful aggression changed everyday life among the victors, and the effect was always to disrupt the family systems that initially produced a surplus of young men of military age. As a result, military expansion and the establishment of colonies on new land by people of a single stock seem never to have endured for more than about six to eight generations. Indeed in some well-attested cases, population decay swiftly took over from population growth. This happened to Athens and Rome, for instance, so that within a couple of centuries of each city's initial expansion, there were no longer enough people of the original citizen stock to populate its immediate hinterland. Slaves were therefore recruited from afar to take over the laborious tasks of cultivation where citizen soldiers once had raised their families.

Exactly what combination of factors checked the expansion of particular populations presumably varied from case to case, and the historical record is incapable of reconstructing details. But in general one can see that successful wars opened new, urban opportunities for the victors; and in proportion as they abandoned the hard life on the land, gathering into cities and spending time in armies, disease exposure intensified due to crowding if nothing else. Simultaneously,

7

soldiers campaigning far from home learned to satisfy their sexual impulses outside of marriage. Under these circumstances, family patterns that had once sustained population growth were sure to weaken at the same time that disease deaths increased. This set rather narrow limits to expansion by simple replication of agricultural communities through military aggression.

Expanding polities that achieved really imperial scale always had to assimilate the conquered into their armies and often found it necessary or convenient to accept recruits from outside imperial borders as well. Thus, the Romans, to cite the case most familiar to us, repeatedly widened the geographical limits of recruitment into their army and in the empire's later days depended on Germans and other foreign auxiliaries to supplement the soldiery available from within the *limes*. The Assyrians had done the same before them, Genghis Khan did the same afterwards, and we may safely assume that all the other great empires of history became great by assimilating hosts of newcomers into the ruling military and administrative elites.

By the eighteenth century, however, when the modern growth of population began, simple aggression by overcrowded rural populations had become impractical. Villagers were enmeshed in a political system that did not usually allow them to indulge in local self-help by forcibly seizing neighboring lands. In a few crevices of European society such old-fashioned responses did find scope. This was the case, for instance, in the western Balkans, where Turkish power was thin on the ground, especially in frontier regions that had been emptied of population by previous wars. Serbian pioneers were therefore able to occupy the Morava valley, south of Belgrade, in course of the eighteenth century. They simply usurped wild forested land, attaining a rude abundance and rate of population growth that resembled life on the American frontier.

When challenged by Turkish authorities, who hoped to

make them into serfs, widespread revolt broke out in 1803. This marked the emergence of the modern Serbian state; but ironically enough, during the nineteenth century, when un-occupied land began to run short, the Serbian government started to enforce private property rights and in doing so dis-rupted the extended families and displaced the local military associations that had allowed the pioneers to defeat the Turks. As a result, after about 1870 Serbian peasants found themselves chafing under the same sort of legal constraints that prevailed in other parts of the Continent.[5]

In most of Europe, access to land—empty or not—was effectually regulated by written entitlements backed by state force. Under these circumstances, collective response to land shortage required revolutionary seizure of power on a na-tionwide scale—an act entirely beyond the capacity of any mere village community. In the absence of the possibility of collective response of a sort that might keep community link-ages intact or even strengthen them—as was happening in Serbia in the eighteenth and early nineteenth centuries—rural families were thrown back on their own resources.

Wherever small holdings predominated, as in France and adjacent regions in the Rhinelands and north Italy, a canny and prudent peasant family might indeed be able to maintain its status and find room in the village for its children as they came of age by purchasing or renting more land and arranging suitable dowries with which to set up the new households. But such successes meant that others had to sell out, thus recruiting new members to an impoverished land-less class that was condemned to live by wage labor, whether in village or in town.

The surge of population growth that set in after 1750 thus put enormous and all but insupportable strain on village communities. Too many extra hands as they came of age had nowhere to go. Towns soon became desperately overcrowded by immigrants seeking a livelihood on the margins of urban society, and in the villages all suitable land was already taken up.[6] It was against this background that the French Revolution broke out and, in its own way, eventually brought an effective solution to the peasant problem.

In the parts of Europe where landlord-managed estates prevailed, circumstances were different. Except in England, high farming, using new crops and techniques, had not spread far from its Netherlandish region of origin in 1750. But when prices were right, conversion to the new husbandry was clearly in the landlord's interest because he could then derive more income from the land. Landlords were usually in a position to override village resistance to change. Moreover, the new husbandry was at least partly also in the interest of the rural poor because its adoption required a good deal of extra work in the fields. Rising grain prices, responding to growing urban numbers and prosperity, came together with a rising labor supply on the land to make the spread of a more intensive style of high farming feasible.[7]

Naturally, the same incentives favoring more intensive cultivation applied to peasant farmers; but in many instances village custom and collective rights inhibited the new, more intensive husbandry. Even when they understood what might be gained by departing from established routines, peasant cultivators were not usually able to persuade or compel their suspicious neighbors to give up traditional rights to pasturing their animals on fallowed and waste lands as high farming required. Landlords commonly could. As a result, French farming lagged far behind the best practice of England and of the Low Countries, as Arthur Young vigorously attested on the very eve of the French Revolution.[8]

Peasant cultivators throughout France and in adjacent regions of north Italy and southwestern Germany thus fell into a nasty trap after about 1750. But where landlords called the tune, adoption of new methods of cultivation could keep pace, more or less, with population growth, thus opening the way for a century of rising productivity on the land and in the cities as well. By far the most important agricultural innovation within reach in 1750 was a change in crop rotation whereby fallow fields were planted with turnips, potatoes, or some other crop that could provide animal and human food. Fodder crops allowed farmers to maintain more animals; more animals meant more manure; and more manure meant better harvests from more richly fertilized fields. Increased yields in turn meant more for sale in the towns, thus allowing urban population to grow at the same time that far more hands were needed to cultivate row crops like turnips and potatoes which had to be hoed once or twice during the growing season to keep down weeds.[9]

As long as gainful employment in towns could be found on a scale sufficient to absorb the portion of the growing population that was not needed in the fields to perform the new tasks of cultivation, countries of the north European plain were therefore in a position to ride the population surge successfully, without imposing unbearable strains on any element of the population.[10] This was in fact what happened between 1750 and 1914, though not before revolution in France had resolved the population problem of the peasant-managed portion of Europe in its own violent but effective fashion.

Let me descend from this level of generalization to look at how the French and English managed the population surge of the late eighteenth century, for the example of these two countries, because they were so successful, became paradigmatic for peoples around the earth during the nineteenth and first part of the twentieth centuries.

A host of circumstances lay behind the French Revolution, and I do not want to leave the impression that population growth was the only thing that mattered. Far from it; but without the deadlock on the land between a growing population and inelastic patterns of cultivation, the course of events could not have been what it was. Peasant unrest provoked the Estates General to "abolish feudalism" on the night of August 4, 1789, for example; and the Paris crowds that propelled the revolution in its early days drew much of their fighting manpower from a floating population of recent migrants from the countryside.[11] The critical role of crowds

11

in the revolutionary dynamic scarcely needs argument; and sure enough, once underemployed and unemployed young men had been drafted into the army and sent off to the frontiers, Parisian crowds lost their fighting spirit. As a result, when Robespierre's adherents sounded the tocsin in 1794, response was weak and ineffectual, and ere long the revolution was over.[12]

In France as a whole, soldiers' deaths came close to canceling out natural increase until 1815; and when Napoleon's armies were disbanded, the veterans who returned to French peasant farms no longer allowed births to run as far ahead of deaths as had happened before they went off to war. Instead, deliberate birth control became widespread, with the result that the French population lagged conspicuously behind the growth rates of adjacent lands throughout the nineteenth century. Why the French behaved differently from other European populations in the nineteenth century is one of the unsolved questions of historical demography. My own favorite idea is to suppose that French family norms altered because so many soldiers returned to rural society after years of exposure to army prostitutes and their ways of preventing unwanted births. No other European nation saw nearly so many long-service veterans return to civil society; and the French veterans returned to a rural society where the motivation for birth control was especially strong because prerevolutionary inelasticities of village custom continued to affect peasant life, making French agricultural productivity lag behind the levels of adjacent parts of Europe down to our own day.[13]

Even though hard times returned to France after 1815, and slow but persistent population growth could only be precariously matched up with access to village land and urban jobs, it still remains true that the revolutionary upheaval solved the problem of too many surplus youths by reducing that surplus violently at first and through changed sexual behavior in the long run. The French thus pioneered what population experts like to call the "demographic transition," by

12

balancing births and deaths again, but at far lower rates than before. Other European lands lagged behind by nearly a century. Lowered birthrates became general only after other wars—primarily World Wars I and II—broke down peasant custom and propagated birth control among the rural populations of all the other European countries, with the sole exception of the Albanian population in Yugoslavia.[14]

In its way, the revolutionary resort to aggressive war resembled the ancient response to land shortage exemplified by the early Roman republic, so much admired by the revolutionaries themselves, though, of course, the French were not so successful as the Romans for they did not colonize conquered lands or rule them for long. It is also true that the lowered birthrates that came to France after 1815 resembled the demographic transition that set in among the Romans after the Hannibalic wars.

But the French Revolution did more than recapitulate Roman precedent. By changing property law and suppressing local privileges and monopolies, the revolutionaries cleared the way for intensification of commercial and industrial activity that proved capable of matching growing numbers with growing wealth down to our own time. This assimilated the French revolutionary recipe for solving the rural crunch of the late eighteenth century to the British response, forming, together, a west European pattern of economic growth based, centrally, upon increasing use of inanimate power for transport and industrial production. This new, or newly expanded, use of inanimate forms of power cheapened goods and increased their quantity; soon it also allowed improvements of quality and the invention of entirely new commodities and devices for human use. A radically new life-style, first for a few, then slowly for larger and larger proportions of the entire population of industrialized countries, thus opened before an astonished world—a transformation of the limits and conditions of human life as radical in its way as the resort to agriculture had been before the dawn of recorded history.

13

This breakthrough was especially spectacular in Britain during the war years 1792–1815, constituting what we are accustomed to call the "industrial revolution." But France was not far behind, and other parts of Europe soon followed suit. No earlier age had seen anything like the increase in power and wealth that new machines and methods of production and transport permitted; and further possibilities have opened up continuously ever since, thanks to fresh inventions and discoveries linking science and technology together.

A firm political frame was essential to western European success. Markets could not function without a legal system that kept internal peace; and operations abroad were much facilitated by state action to protect trade, using force if necessary. The governments of France and Britain had lent themselves to these purposes far more energetically than most others even before the middle of the eighteenth century. Political transformations after 1789 therefore merely extended and confirmed the willingness of both governments to protect and encourage privately managed industrial and commercial enterprises, while taxing them lightly enough to allow continued expansion.

Bitter rivalry between the two nations had the further effect of rallying popular support for policies at home that helped the rich more obviously than the poor, while reinforcing a sense of common identity that sustained aggressive actions abroad, especially when a given advance seemed likely to forestall some success for the other nation. Within the European state system as a whole—presently reinforced by new national players like Italy and Germany—the effect was to magnify European power compared with other peoples and civilizations. The tangible evidence of Europe's new advantage over others was the ease with which small expeditionary forces sufficed to open markets and build colonial empires that extended across most of Africa and much of Asia by 1914.[15]

The role of population growth in sustaining the

14

nineteenth-century expansion of Europe was obvious and scarcely needs arguing. Demographic takeoff, as background of the economic transformation of Great Britain from 1750 to 1850, is a familiar theme among historians of the industrial revolution.[16] Assuredly, without the impulsion of growing numbers, upsetting older equilibria everywhere, the pace of British economic development would have been slower. It is equally obvious that new urban jobs, coupled with continued agricultural improvement and a safety valve in the form of increasingly easy emigration overseas, permitted rapid population growth to persist in Great Britain until after 1870 without provoking the sort of impasse that had undergirded the revolution in France.

But, as the duke of Wellington is said to have remarked about the battle of Waterloo, it was a damned close run thing. London crowds had foreshadowed the actions of Parisian crowds during the so-called Gordon Riots of 1780.[17] Subsequently, British patriotism and resistance to the revolution became too closely connected to allow contagion from across the Channel; but very rapid population growth, more than double the French rate during the first decades of the nineteenth century, put intense strain on English society.[18] No general rise in the living standard of the working classes occurred until the 1850s; and conditions for the poor remained truly desperate long after that, clustered as they were in hideous urban slums.

Nevertheless, public relief in times of dearth and continued expansion of rural and urban productivity through a long series of technical changes did keep British society from revolution *à la française* and eventually allowed new wealth to percolate down to a growing proportion of the entire population. Simultaneously, British power among the nations skyrocketed, as British agents opened new markets for machine-made goods in distant lands and set the pace for European expansion around the globe.

Great Britain enjoyed entirely exceptional advantages. Located on the ocean face of a crowded Europe, the British were protected from direct military threat by their insular position and could dispatch settlers as well as goods across the seas more or less at will, because in the nineteenth century no power on earth could rival the Royal Navy. Yet despite these unique advantages, important parts of the British Isles had no share in the nation's industrial success. This was conspicuously true of Ireland, where an already poverty-stricken peasantry faced starvation in 1845–46 when blight, freshly come from South America, ruined the potato crop. Millions had come to depend on the potato for almost all their nourishment. Its almost complete destruction was therefore catastrophic and precipitated more than a century of population shrinkage.

The Irish case points up the unusual character of the contrary experience in most parts of Britain. Why did English population not pond back in the countryside and learn to live on a diet of potatoes, as the Irish did? One factor, surely, was widespread prejudice against the Irish who migrated to Britain in sufficient numbers to constitute a distinct underclass from the eighteenth century onwards. The Gordon Riots of 1780 were, in fact, aimed at keeping the Irish in their place, subject to special legal disabilities as Catholics. Protestant Englishmen did all they could to avoid sinking to the Irish level, and one of the important outward signs was refusal to depend on a potato diet. English countrymen were spared that indignity in most of the English shires because under the so-called Speenhamland system for poor relief, payments were keyed to the price of bread. The English poor therefore never became as destitute as the Irish or as vulnerable to the failure of a single crop.

Even so, one wonders what set England and Lowland Scotland off on such a different path from that followed by Ireland and the Scottish Highlands, for the Highlands, like Ireland, were overrun in the early nineteenth century by a poverty-stricken tenantry eking out a bare existence from patches of land planted with potatoes and little else. Improving landlords of the sort who were expanding high farming across England and Germany during the nineteenth century had little success in Ireland. Their efforts required massive clearances of surplus population—acts bitterly resented and effectively resisted by boycott and acts of vandalism against landlord property and, occasionally, against persons as well. And in the Highlands, where landlords did prevail, they ended up by destroying the old clan society entirely, substituting sheep runs and grouse moors for subsistence farms.

Improving landlords, keen to respond to market prices, were therefore no guarantee of successful development; and dependence on potatoes did not guarantee an Irish level of poverty either, as the experience of the Continent showed. In course of the nineteenth century, potatoes did come to provide the staple nourishment of the lower classes from Belgium eastward across the north European plain, but throughout these lands potato culture fitted into new crop rotations required by commercialized high framing and so helped to facilitate a more general commercial and industrial development.[19] Yet simultaneously, and within a few hundred miles of London, the most active center of world commerce, the same crop reinvigorated subsistence farming in Ireland and set the stage for a harsh collision between landlords and tenants whose competing claims for right and justice distracted British politics until after World War I.

The unhappy way Irish population growth occurred within a society where subsistence and commercial agricultural production overlapped each other was replicated on the other flank of Europe. Beginning in the late eighteenth century, Romanian peasants came to depend on maize as completely as the Irish depended on potatoes. Maize was another American newcomer, and in the warm and well-watered parts of Danubian Europe it increased calorie yields per acre almost as much as the potato did in the cooler north. (It was also a suitable substitute for fallow, because hoeing during the growing season was necessary for maize as well as for potatoes.) Unlike the Irish, Romanian peasants were legally tied to the soil as serfs until 1864; but they were like the Irish

17

inasmuch as they lived as subsistence farmers on a food that urban populations disdained, while simultaneously laboring on land owned by (mostly absentee) landlords producing wheat and meat for distant urban markets—in this instance centered not in London but in Constantinople.

In one respect, Romanians were worse off, for a diet of maize brings on a deficiency disease known as pellagra, whereas Irishmen, nourished almost exclusively by potatoes, enjoyed vigorous health. Perhaps for that reason, Romanian peasants were slow to organize any kind of political protest against their lot; and when rural discontent did become apparent, it took an anti-Semitic direction. This is not really surprising, for Jews played a prominent role as estate agents for absent landlords and also engaged in petty trade with the peasantry—transactions in which the peasants commonly felt cheated.[20]

Thus one sees how commercialization of agriculture and intensified land use collided nastily with subsistence forms of rural life in the two flanks of Europe; and how population growth had the effect of creating an impoverished and resentful peasantry, exposed to sudden catastrophe in Ireland and to chronic malnourishment in Romania.

We are liable to think that the successful responses in the core areas of Europe were somehow normal, and that these failures on the fringes were exceptional. Because it was the successful countries that enjoyed new access to power and wealth in the nineteenth and twentieth centuries, their role expanded, and world history came to turn very largely on what their citizens and officials tried to do in other lands. The expanded productivity—both agricultural and industrial— and the no less expanded role for the national state that emerged from the industrial and French revolutions therefore became a model for other peoples everywhere. In that sense, one is perhaps justified in supposing that the west European response to the modern growth of population was a norm. But it was a norm to which others aspired, not one they achieved, save in rare and exceptional cases. The delicate balance between rural and urban productivity and concerted public action that sustained Europe's primacy in the world was difficult to replicate—so difficult that only Japan and some lands of European settlement overseas, most notably the United States of America, succeeded in doing so, at least until very recently indeed.

This at least suggests that what happened in western Europe was altogether exceptional, if not quite miraculous.[21] By 1914 the Continent was supporting almost three times as many people as it had boasted in 1700, and a good many of them enjoyed a much higher standard of living than their ancestors had done. In addition, between 1800 and 1914 about forty million European emigrants had settled overseas in the Americas, South Africa, Australia, and Oceania. Together with some ten million Russian pioneers who moved south and east into the Caucasus and Siberia, these European emigrants brought vast tracts of fertile land under cultivation, thus scattering outliers of what we have learned to call Western Civilization around the entire globe.[22] Growing populations at home accelerated this expansion, and, in turn, successful expansion allowed population growth to persist into the twentieth century. In this obvious sense, Europe's political response to the new demographic regime of modern times conformed to ancient precedent, but on a vastly enlarged scale.

Yet even so, Europe's nineteenth-century pace of population growth was capable of outrunning local resources and provoking new political crises. By all odds the greatest of these crises was precipitated by a population crunch among the South Slavs. The onset of demographic difficulty in the modern area of Yugoslavia began in the 1870s. It was marked by guerrilla outbreaks in Bosnia and Herzegovina in 1876 and in Macedonia after 1903, by a rush of emigration to America from about 1880 in provinces near the Adriatic, and by intensified nationalist and socialist agitation among those who stayed behind.

Revolutionary ideologies were nothing new. Such no-tions had simmered beneath the surface of European society at least since the adoption of Christianity with its millenarian hopes. As far as the Balkans were concerned, revolutionary ideals had begun to take modern secular form in the late eighteenth century and in due time inspired or at least helped to provoke the Greek Revolution of 1821. But from the 1870s revolutionary aspirations—suitably updated and modernized—acquired new driving force among village youths who could neither find satisfactory careers in town nor live in their native villages as their forefathers had done because there was not enough land to go round anymore.

A generation earlier, in 1848, when revolutionary hopes attracted at least temporary support among many urban dwellers, the resulting disturbances of public order in central Europe were brief and superficial. The crop failures of 1845–46 failed to set the countryside in motion as bad crop years in France before 1789 had done, because throughout almost all of the Germanic regions of Europe, the spread of high farming sufficed to maintain a viable balance between numbers, work, and land. But in the decades before 1914 rural discontent became general in the northern Balkans and in somewhat less acute form affected the rest of eastern Europe as well.

This set the stage for World War I; and the life of Gavrilo Princip, whose pistol shot triggered the conflict, was aptly paradigmatic. Born in a poor village of Bosnia, he was one of nine children, of whom six died in infancy. As second son, Gavrilo had to seek his fortune away from home, and his halfhearted pursuit of formal qualification for state employment by attending secondary schools eventually provoked a break with his family. Instead of finding a place within the hierarchy of an extended family, as his ancestors had done, Princip joined a floating population of revolutionaries who espoused the ideal of South Slav brotherhood—a brotherhood (very imperfectly) approximated by the café life-style the youthful revolutionaries formed for themselves.[23]

World War I had other roots, of course, and one may

even believe that the rural difficulties of eastern Europe were mere background noise against which Great Power rivalries played themselves out. Yet the statesmanship of the Great Powers surely reflected the aggressive politics of expanding populations that had been practiced with such success by Britain, France, and Russia throughout the nineteenth century, and which Germans and Austrians very much wanted to emulate in the twentieth.

But, as in ancient times, so too in ours: the decades since World War I seem to show that the demographic underpinning of aggressive politics is self-limiting in our time just as it was in antiquity. European population growth slacked off, first in the west, and since World War II, also in the east. This is a fundamental reversal. Birth control now prevails throughout Europe, and if recent trends should continue, instead of growing, Europe's populations will soon begin to shrink. Even if that does not happen, sharply reduced rates of natural increase signal a new demographic era which may be expected to find its own distinctive political expressions. Before exploring these novelties, however, the politics of growing populations as manifested in the rest of the world, where prevailing circumstances made successful responses to rising populations far more difficult than was the case in Europe, deserve our attention.

2

THE POLITICS OF
EXPANDING POPULATIONS:
BEYOND EUROPE

In the first chapter I suggested that west European nations responded to the modern growth of population by undergoing a fundamental mutation and finding a new technological-ecological niche for themselves. Rising numbers were matched by rising agricultural productivity and by even more spectacular increases of industrial productivity, elevating Europe's wealth and power beyond all previous limits and allowing European nations to pursue a politics of expansion around the world.

This extraordinary achievement had ambiguous impact elsewhere. In a few places other peoples found it possible to treat the European mutation as a model to be imitated, with appropriate local divergences and differences. But successful imitation was unusual, being confined to Japan and some lands of European settlement overseas—our own country chief among them. More often, increasing numbers failed to provoke anything like the new style of industrialized society that dominated the European and world scene, either because local institutions and aptitudes were resistant, or because Europeans, having seized privileged positions for themselves, constricted and constrained local initiatives.

Consequently, the diversity within Europe itself, whereby Ireland and Romania went one way while England

and Germany went another, was more than replicated elsewhere. Each country and district wrestled in its own way
with the new circumstances that population growth provoked. Amidst such wide variability, choice of where to focus
attention must be arbitrary, though it need not be entirely
random. Sampling extremes may perhaps illumine the process as a whole, though we ought not to lose sight of the
commonalities that pervaded all the divergent responses to
population growth.

Let me start with two observations about commonalities. First of all, the rule of thumb whereby growing populations may be expected to sustain a politics of expansion
seems well enough borne out by events since 1750, even
though Asian and African peoples seldom had much success
in their efforts at expansion. Instead, their resort to violence,
when it was not protective of old ways and aimed against
intrusive Europeans, was likely to be aimed at domestic foes,
as when the Taipings attacked the Manchu rulers of China
and their Chinese collaborators. Peoples of Europe, when
they lacked a national state of their own, behaved in quite
the same way, as the internal conflicts of the Hapsburg, Ro-
manov, and Ottoman empires may remind us.

Everything depended on where discontented populations drew the line between "us" and "them." Criteria for
this distinction between friend and foe were potentially infi-
nite. In fact, finding new social identities and achieving a satisfactory life within their often competing demands were
basic problems for all those whose traditional ways of life in
the countryside became insupportable when land ran short.
Large and inclusive identities, such as the nation-states into
which Europe coalesced, were more promising units than
family, village, region, tribe, or class inasmuch as the exchanges upon which the new industrial-commercial style of
society depended flourished best on a large scale, permitting
millions of persons to act more or less harmoniously while
keeping the public peace.

But building inclusive new nations was difficult among

24

populations divided by regional, tribal, sectarian, linguistic, and occupational identities. Old and new moral commitments were usually in conflict, making it difficult for distressed and fragmented populations to act wholeheartedly and effectively when seeking to express their expansive tendencies and hopes. Nonetheless, the impulse to occupy new niches, roles, and territory was ever present, because no other policy seemed in the least likely to solve the practical difficulties that faced an overnumerous rural population. When overt force was impractical, infiltration and subterfuge served instead.

The other commonality that united European and non-European peoples under the new regime that population growth imposed was the erosion of a long-standing social and psychological barrier between town and country. Throughout recorded history, townsmen imposed and profited from government and an established orthodoxy of thought and act, while rural folk submitted with whatever grace they could. But, liberty, equality, and fraternity within separate nations, as worked out in post-1789 Europe, meant the gradual mobilization of peasants as citizens, soldiers, and voters in their own right.[1] Not all European governments had managed to make peasant participation in politics a routine ongoing process before 1914; and the political mobilization of the peasantries of Asia and Africa scarcely got under way until after World War I.

But by now, the rural majority of humankind has begun to entertain political aspirations; and no really large rural populations remain indifferent, subordinated, and inert as aforetime. Crowding on the land means that the old routines of daily life have come very widely into question, so that political leaders and programs must offer a plausible recipe for escaping from an unacceptable prospect of impoverishment. Radical new ideas about what is right and possible are readily at hand because new modes of communication—radio, TV, and audio tapes—can now cross political boundaries and penetrate even to once remote villages.

25

Hitherto, civilization has been based on exploitation of the rural majority. Within the boundaries of a few industrialized countries subsistence farming is now no more, and the ancient inequity between town and country has in fact been transcended. But within the world as a whole, peasants and ex-peasants persist in their billions, poised on the margins of commercialized society and seeking access to townspeople's privileges and comforts. Enormous risks and enormous possibilities inhere in such a posture. The human majority is stirring around the entire globe for the first time in history. This makes our age different from any that has gone before.

Even if peasant political aspirations for full equality and perfect liberty fail to be realized, as innumerable localized peasant revolts have failed in the past, the worldwide character of this movement makes return to the old basis of civilized society seem improbable. Like steam heating up in a closed space, the world's peasantries may only provoke a scalding explosion; but as we saw actually did happen in Europe, their articulation into a market system may also in suitable circumstances activate powerful new engines for the creation of wealth. No James Watt has yet figured out how to produce wealth and forestall scalding explosions everywhere and every time that rural population pressure becomes critical. Nonetheless, the old system of society whereby most people toiled in the fields for subsistence and parted with a portion of their product as taxes and rents without getting anything more tangible than protection in return seems unlikely to revive. Subordination, submission, and inequality may not disappear; but any future social system, to be viable, will have to make agricultural production and distribution part of a larger system of exchanging goods and services. Nothing less can hold its own in competition with the already industrialized societies that have in fact made producers of food into citizens.

These commonalities, however real, still permit enormous variation in actual political behavior. An obvious puzzle, when one contemplates the world as a whole, is that

26

some peoples have multiplied enormously without experiencing more than superficial political upheavals. Java is a case in point, and so is Egypt. Others have suffered decades of revolution—China most conspicuously. And then there is the case of Japan, where a pair of revolutions from the top, first in 1867 and then in 1945, twice worked wonders and did so in an amazingly short period of time. Moreover, in the frontier lands of Eurasia and overseas, where almost uninhabited territories were still awaiting settlement in 1750, rapidly growing populations pursued a spectacularly successful politics of expansion but did so under widely different regimes and with contrasting results to date.

Let me say something first about the contrasts of the frontier, because in these lands the factors affecting paths of political development seem relatively simple and straightforward.

The really extraordinary circumstance was the existence in 1750 of vast thinly populated regions which were, nonetheless, well fitted for agriculture and other human uses. This situation resulted from epidemiological disasters of enormous magnitude that had occurred in immediately preceding centuries. Millions of Amerindians died when exposed to European and then to African diseases, and destruction persisted wherever white traders and pioneers penetrated Indian country. As penicillin mold on a nutritive jelly clears a path for its own growth by exuding a chemical that kills off bacteria, so settlers of European and African descent, simply by breathing in the presence of disease-inexperienced Indians, provoked repeated epidemics that cleared the way for their continued advance.[2]

Even within the confines of the Old World, where disease gradients were less extreme, a new exposure to bubonic plague had depopulated the western steppelands after the middle of the fourteenth century, creating another almost empty frontier zone into which Russian and Polish pioneers began to move after about 1550.

Epidemiological disruption of previously isolated populations was nothing new. It had helped Eurasian civilizations to encroach on their neighbors for many centuries. But in modern times the scale of the phenomenon was magnified enormously because, as I argued in chapter 1, civilized populations had become so disease-saturated as to be nearly proof against serious epidemic and at the same time commanded improved means of transport so that no part of the habitable world remained beyond their reach. Consequently, within the Old World, Siberian forests suffered radical depopulation beginning in the sixteenth century as the steppe-lands had done earlier, while overseas the native inhabitants of Australia, southernmost Africa, and the islands of Oceania were ravaged in the same way that the Americas were being ravaged. Everywhere, the net of communications that first Mongol horsemen and then European sailors had woven round the earth was drawn tighter; and as contacts multiplied, exposure to lethal infections among disease-inexperienced populations increased, often to their utter destruction and always to their enormous disadvantage in trying to resist disease-experienced strangers who were already well adapted—both biologically and culturally—to the infections they brought with them.[3]

The modern demographic regime that resulted from juxtaposition of expanding populations in the Eurasian heartlands with emptying frontier zones offered an extraordinary opportunity for European expansion, because to begin with, Europeans had a near monopoly of transoceanic shipping. Colonists in the temperate parts of America and elsewhere overseas multiplied with quite exceptional rapidity once a few initial adjustments to the new environment had been made—reliance on maize instead of wheat as the staple crop being the critical change for North America. Russian pioneers in the Ukraine, Caucasus, and western Siberia exhibited similar rates of natural increase without having to alter traditional agricultural methods in any significant way. Yet as we all know, the political character of North American society diverged from the European norm by becoming freer and more egalitarian, whereas the Russians submitted to harsher subordination with less personal and civic freedom than other Europeans enjoyed.

This contrast is only superficially surprising. Frontier societies, in fact, always exhibited both extremes. Slavery was, after all, very prominent in the Americas and lasted until 1888 in Brazil;[4] and some Russian pioneers lived quite as rude and free a life as Daniel Boone ever did in Kentucky. What tipped the balance between freedom and subordination in Russia was the urgency of military defense arising from Russia's exposed geographical position. For centuries, Tartar slaving raids were a serious danger to settlers in the Ukraine. Early efforts at self-defense were overtaken in the course of the eighteenth century by the superior effectiveness of regular troops, trained in the European manner and supported by heavy taxation of the Russian people at large and of the peasantry in particular. Then, after the reforms of Peter the Great (1869–1725) gave the Russians military superiority over their Polish, Swedish, and Ottoman rivals, the imperial army was able to push Russian frontiers far ahead of pioneer settlements. Ere long, disease-experienced Moslem populations of central Asia came under the Russian yoke, though not until after Russian proconsuls had defined a frontier with China (Treaties of Nerchinsk, 1689, Kiakhta, 1727) that gave the eastern steppelands to the Chinese and reserved the forests north of the Amur River for the Russians.

Thereafter, although residues of frontier freedom survived in remoter regions of Siberia, throughout most of the Russian lands peasants were legally classed as serfs and were compelled to send some of their sons to serve the czar in the army, while the rest served their aristocratic masters within limits set by the vigorously egalitarian institutions of the village community itself.[5] Wholesale compulsion was required to maintain the military-bureaucratic system that had made Russia great; and even after Russia's failures in the Crimean War (1854–56) showed some of the defects of legal compulsion, efforts to incorporate the peasant majority into the Russian body politic by abolishing serfdom in 1861 and giving peasants the vote in 1906 quite failed to overcome the heritage of rigorous subordination to the dictates of a small elite—a tradition that continues to prevail down to the present.

It is worth remarking that what gave the Russian imperial system its continued vitality for a century or so after 1750 was the increasing flow of tax revenues resulting from a rapid commercialization of agriculture. Noble landowners compelled their serfs to raise grain for sale in distant markets, thereby providing themselves with enough money to live like European gentlemen (more or less) and providing the state with sufficient monies to pay its officials and soldiers. The commercial basis of east European serfdom sustained wholesale resort to compulsory labor long after Russia's need for defense against neighbors ceased to be really urgent. The commercialization of Russian agriculture meant therefore that Russian society tended to assimilate itself to the plantation regimes that characterized much of the Americas, where frontier inequality also prevailed.

The freedom and equality we like to associate with the American frontier actually prevailed only where agricultural production for export did not develop on a big scale and where settlers of European descent displaced the native inhabitants so completely as to create ethnically and culturally more or less homogeneous communities. Wherever, instead, large numbers of Indians survived, or slaves from Africa took over the heavy work of plantation agriculture, laminated polyethnic societies arose in which those of European descent lorded it over others. Under these circumstances, special legal arrangements (slavery, peonage) reinforced white dominion in much the same way that Russian law separated noblemen from serfs.

As time passed and populations grew, mestizos and mulattoes multiplied and came to constitute a majority in lands where the whites had turned themselves into a managerial and ruling class. This cushioned the stark distinction between

30

master and servant, and as landscapes filled up, the need for special legal compulsion to get nasty work done diminished. The abolition of slavery and peonage, when it came in the course of the nineteenth century, like the abolition of serfdom in Russia, therefore did not make a great deal of difference, at least to begin with. Liberated slaves like liberated serfs had little choice but to continue to work on the land as they had done before, even if their legal circumstance had altered.

Nevertheless, in the longer run legal freedom within a market economy created new risks and possibilities. In Russia, after considerable development of modern industry and such landmark changes as the construction of railroads, social differentiation along European lines set in. This created new strains in the villages, where old ideas requiring everyone to share the burdens of servitude equally made profit from buying and selling seem selfish and unjust. Such discontents were intensified in parts of central Russia by mounting pressure on the land and were then enormously reinforced by governmental failures during World War I.[6]

As a result, the majority of the Russian peasantry backed the Bolshevik Revolution in 1917 and ten years later found themselves subjected to a party dictatorship that aimed to industrialize the country by command. As long as an ample supply of underemployed rural labor could be tapped to build factories and then tend the new assembly lines, the Bolshevik recipe for industrialization by command worked well enough, even though it often wasted manpower and materials. Recently, the pool of underemployed rural labor has run dry, and a precipitate decay of Russian birthrates makes the wasteful use of labor too costly to be borne with equanimity. Consequently, the Russians seem, as they were once before in the middle of the nineteenth century, face to face with the question of how to escape from their heritage of political authoritarianism and rigorous social subordination in order to catch up with the wealth, power, and economic efficiency attained by the freer and more egalitarian societies of western Europe and America.

The eventual closure of the frontier in North America had the effect of modifying the stark initial bifurcation between frontier equality and subsistence farming on the one hand and an enslaved work force for commercial production on the other. By degrees urban society replicated European occupational differentiations; and as we all know, when need for defense against the French disappeared after 1763, thirteen of the fifteen English colonies in North America won their independence after declaring it in 1776. Thereafter, the United States went from strength to strength, lagging only a little behind the European development of modern industrialism and pursuing the politics of territorial expansion with the same sort of easy success in reaching for the Pacific across an entire continent that the Russians had experienced in crossing Siberia about a century before.

We often take our national past as normative. But in other overseas frontier lands, the population growth and political development of the past 250 years have produced quite different upshots. South Africa is an obvious example, for there efforts to maintain and reinforce white supremacy have created a three-tiered society with different legal rights for Asians and "coloureds," blacks, and whites.

In other ex-frontier lands, great diversity prevails. In the parts of America where large Amerindian populations existed when Columbus arrived, survivors and mixed bloods gradually became more and more disease-experienced, with the result that initial die-offs slowed to a halt, and eventually population growth to match that of the immigrant white and black populations set in among them. Thus, for example, the population of the Aztec heartland in central Mexico bottomed out about 130 years after the initial disease disaster had occurred. A painfully slow initial recovery then gradually gave way to the rapid population growth that continues to our own day. In other regions, where contacts with invading whites got under way later, population turnaround was correspondingly delayed. In time, the balance of numbers and morale in the countryside turned decisively against the managerial class of whites, with the result that in our own century a series of revolutionary movements overturned landlord regimes in Mexico, Peru, and most of the lands between.

In northern Brazil and on the islands of the Caribbean, African slaves played a larger role than in most parts of the mainland. As long as sugar plantations remained profitable and fresh slaves could be imported freely, harsh conditions of life and a great imbalance of numbers between male and female made natural increase impossible for the slave populations of most of the sugar islands. Nonetheless, Africans and their descendants could withstand the tropical diseases like yellow fever and malaria that had come with the slave ships better than others; and after the turn of the nineteenth century, as the ruthlessness of exploitation diminished, black and mulatto populations began to sustain themselves and then to grow.[7] In Brazil, black, white, and red (together with a significant number of Japanese immigrants) mingled in different proportions in different parts of the country to produce a unique and distinctive society, dominated still by its white element but generally a good deal less color-conscious than is true in the United States.[8]

In the Caribbean, successful black rebellion dates back to the beginning of the nineteenth century in Haiti, but each island had its own history, and in some of them landlord regimes still survive. Often plantation agriculture collapsed when profits from sugar disappeared at about the same time that slavery was abolished (1833 in British, 1848 in French colonies), whereupon liberated slaves were left more or less to their own devices to create whatever basis for subsistence they found possible. In Cuba, on the other hand, sugar plantations and the abolition of slavery (1886) both came late, and the black population remained a minority. Radical revolution, aimed partly against economic and other interests of the United States, was correspondingly delayed until after Fidel Castro came to power in 1959.

The descendants of black slaves in Brazil and the Caribbean islands, like the rural Indian and mestizo populations of

Mexico, Peru, and other Latin American states, have not entered into modern industrial-commercial exchange networks
very successfully, yet their numbers are growing at a very
rapid rate so that in more and more localities old-fashioned
subsistence farming has become inadequate to sustain the
population at accustomed standards of living. Dispossession
of landlords and disruption of plantation production under
foreign management have not sufficed to relieve hardship on
the land. Even the most enthusiastic revolutionaries, whether
in Mexico (1911), Cuba (1959), or Nicaragua (1979), have
not solved the problem of too many people for existing economic niches. Emigrants crowd out of the countryside and
swarm into urban slums without finding new jobs to match
their numbers. Radical dissatisfaction results, and it is not
surprising that guerrilla violence has already appeared in
Peru and El Salvador and simmers just beneath the surface in
neighboring countries as well.

In all these lands, the gap between town and country
remains wide and deep; and inherited cultural divergences
among ethnic groups add another divisive element. The notion that historical development will sooner or later bring
such societies into line with the model of modernity we cher-
ish in the United States seems implausible. Responses to economic and political possibilities are always conditioned by
circumstance and by cultural heritages; and these being diverse, the responses will surely continue to be diverse, even in
so tightly interconnected a world as ours.[9]

So much for the diverse political expressions that accompanied population growth in what are now merely ex-
frontier lands. In general, immigration and natural increase
of population have now repaired the gash in human occu-
pancy of the earth that was caused by the massive epidemics
of the early modern era. We are now more nearly one world,
and the differences between the older centers of civilized life
and the former frontier lands are far less than they used to
be. Hence the politics of population growth no longer differs
systematically between heartlands and periphery as was the

34

case when empty land abounded on the frontier and hands were scarce.

Turning attention next to those heartlands, I propose first to compare China and Japan because their different responses to the modern growth of population constituted opposite and extreme cases. Then I will glance at countries where growing rural populations seem to have descended into poverty without resorting to massive or prolonged political violence, and ask, why? This leaves out all the halfway houses and intermediate cases, but at least it suggests the spectrum of political responses to runaway population growth that have manifested themselves so far.

The marked divergence between China and Japan in the way they coped with growing populations after about 1750 seems especially surprising because, to the untutored eye, their starting points seem very similar. Rice paddies were the most important form of agriculture in both countries, and where they prevailed, fields were small and population was exceedingly dense owing to the exceptional productivity of paddy fields and the immense labor required for maintaining and preparing the ground, managing water supplies, and then transplanting, weeding, and harvesting the rice. Where climate allowed, paddies produced a second crop each year, and three crops a year were sometimes achieved in the longer growing seasons of the extreme south. Moreover, commercial agriculture was widespread in both countries. It was older and perhaps not growing much any more in China, whereas commercialized farming was newer and still expanding within Japan. Nearly always nuclear families did the actual farming, but rights to land were complex and various— ownership being sometimes diffused within extended lineages. A great variety of sharecropping and wage labor agreements further complicated village relationships, while tax obligations were sometimes met collectively by the village as a whole and sometimes collected from individual owners.[10]

Deliberate restraints on multiplication of numbers already prevailed among Japanese and (at least some) Chinese

35

peasants also. Marriages were often delayed until the new-lyweds had a prospect of access to enough land to support a family; and infanticide, especially of females, sometimes skewed the sex ratio quite drastically.[11] Yet the population of China rose from somewhere between 200 and 250 million in 1750 to no less than 1,059 million in 1985, while the population of Japan grew from about 26 million in 1750 to 120 million in 1985.[12] The Chinese figures stagger the imagination; but it is noteworthy that despite their very different economic and political history since 1750, the population of each country increased by almost the same proportion— about halfway between four and five times over.

China's political experience of rising numbers divided into two very different eras. Until 1796, the Manchu dynasty did what one might expect of a government presiding over an expanding population. Having consolidated military control within Manchuria and China itself by about 1684, China's diplomats and armies launched a vigorous and successful expansion across every landward frontier, establishing imperial suzerainty and varying degrees of administrative control over Mongolia, Turkestan, Tibet, Nepal, Burma, and Annam. Settlers followed in the wake of the armies wherever suitable land existed; but in practice the main frontiers open to Chinese colonization were in the southwest where various hill peoples were displaced by Chinese cultivators and in the northeast where, however, the Manchus wished to preserve pasturelands for their own use and so prohibited Chinese immigrants from penetrating beyond a frontier fixed in the southern part of Manchuria.

Chinese pioneers were therefore quite unable to match the record of west European settlers overseas and fell far short of what Russians were doing in the western steppes during the same centuries simple because the eastern steppe-lands within their reach were too dry and cold to allow agriculture to flourish as it could in the Ukraine, Caucasus, and parts of Siberia. Beyond the reach of the imperial authorities, Chinese traders and artisans were active in much of southeast

Asia; but there, too, Chinese opportunities were limited, on the one hand by competition with local peoples and, on the other, by a growing European predominance in large-scale commerce that reflected their initial monopoly of new technologies of manufacture and transport. Thus China's initial responses to population growth, spectacularly successful though they looked at the time, still fell short of matching contemporary European achievements, partly for geographical reasons and partly for institutional, social, and cultural reasons.[13]

Having thus fallen short, China presently descended into civil strife. Disorders became serious in 1796; subsequent repression restored a precarious peace, which broke down again in 1850 when the Taiping rebellion spread throughout the heartland of south-central China and raged for fourteen years. Defeat at the hands of comparatively trifling European expeditionary forces, beginning with the Opium War of 1841–42, added to the government's troubles; and efforts at self-strengthening, though eventually victorious against the Taipings, could not prevent recurrent domestic uprisings and continued foreign aggression. The overthrow of the dynasty in 1911 did nothing to mend matters; only after further decades of civil and foreign war, 1927–49, did China regain full sovereignty and achieve internal peace, within somewhat reduced boundaries. (Taiwan separated; China's rather shadowy suzerainty over Burma, Nepal, and Annam was not restored; and territories to the south of the Amur, ceded to Russia in 1860, remained part of the Soviet Union.)[14]

Communist rule has remained firmly in place since 1949, and forty years of domestic peace may well have inaugurated a new era for China. Nevertheless, the so-called Great Leap Forward (1958–62), swiftly followed by the Cultural Revolution (1966–77) and the army's repression of the student protests in 1989, verged on officially sanctioned renewals of civil strife. Resulting dislocations were severe enough to provoke famine and many millions of deaths.[15] No one can suppose that China has yet brought population and

37

resources into anything like a stable balance; and if recent draconian efforts to limit births to one per family were to succeed (as seems not to be the case), the nation would soon confront a different but equally unendurable demographic difficulty when today's parents grow old, leaving an inadequate number of offspring to try to support them.

Japan escaped China's tribulations. Instead, its accommodation to a rising population conformed, outwardly at least, to the European pattern of national integration, industrialization, and political expansion. Beginning in 1867, revolutionaries rallied under the aegis of the emperor to abolish the shogunate, along with traditional fiefdoms and samurai privileges. Within ten years, the sporadic public disorders that accompanied these changes ended. Peasants became obedient taxpayers and soldiers. Agricultural productivity increased as population grew, and surplus rural youths found more or less adequate urban employment.

From the start, the reformers focused their efforts on attaining military strength and embarked on territorial expansion as early as 1869 when they organized colonization of the thinly occupied northern island of Hokkaido and then gained title to Okinawa in 1874. Korea came next, but Japanese intervention there provoked a war with China in 1894–95. Japan triumphed, and the peace transferred sovereignty over Taiwan and the Pescadores to Japan's growing empire. That was followed, a decade later, by an even more spectacular victory over the Russians in Manchuria, 1904–5, and the acquisition of southern Sakhalin. Korea was annexed in 1910, and during World War 1 Japan staked a claim to special rights in China, then withdrew under American and European diplomatic pressure, only to advance again after 1931, when the Japanese army set up a puppet regime in Manchuria and then invaded China proper in 1937. The Japanese then carved out a still more ambitious "Co-Prosperity Sphere," embracing all of southeast Asia and the southwest Pacific in 1941–42; but catastrophic military defeat brought the Japanese empire to an abrupt end in 1945. All this matched European behavior very closely; and the collapse of the Japanese overseas empire in 1945, as it turned out, simply prefigured the post-World War II disruption of European colonial empires.

Population pressure as a factor in Japan's imperial career was obvious. Need for land and resources was part of the official justification for military aggression; and in fact, in 1940, 2.9 million Japanese civilians were living abroad, mostly in managerial positions within Japan's imperial dependencies, and another million were serving in the armed forces overseas. One calculation holds that this emigration reduced the number of men of military age in Japan itself by 8 percent.[16] Such a diminution constituted a not insignificant safety valve for rural restlessness, which simmered in the background of Japanese public life during the depression years of the 1930s.

The American occupation after 1945 brought a new revolution from the top in its train, aimed above all at extirpating Japanese militarism. Success, so far at least, seems to have been as rapid and complete as the success of the earlier revolution in launching imperial expansion. Land reform, transferring ownership of farmland to those who tilled the soil, was a part of the postwar revolution from above and helped to relieve discontent in the villages. More important was renewed and spectacular expansion of urban activity, lasting to the present and making Japan by far the most successful country of the postwar world in matters of industry, commerce, and finance.

It seems, therefore, that Japan found satisfactory niches for its expanding population throughout the extraordinary growth of the past 250 years, partly by straightforward military-political expansion, but more significantly by dint of intensified agricultural productivity at home, and, most spectacularly of all, by industrial and commercial triumphs at home and abroad. Recently, a postwar drop in birthrates promises to stabilize Japanese population in the very near future and may even, as has already happened in some European countries, lead to population shrinkage. It thus appears that Japan profited from the modern surge of population to increase its wealth and power enormously, matching anything European nations achieved without the advantage of a head start and without having access to empty frontier lands as the Europeans did.

It is an amazing record that discredits simple dependency theory because Japan most emphatically escaped dependence on outside powers, despite initial limitations put on Japan's sovereignty by treaties giving Europeans and Americans extraterritorial rights. Instead, a long series of triumphs in the international marketplace allowed Japan to make other countries, most notably the United States, dependent on loans from Japan.

Japan's success is especially remarkable because of the contrast with China's long-drawn-out civil strife. What explains such a difference? Somehow the Japanese managed to maintain local cohesion while willingly accepting subordination to and cooperation with a nationwide central authority. They therefore were able to act together efficiently both in economic and political affairs. Because most were peasants to begin with, this required the survival of village solidarities, hierarchies, and identities and the transfer of village habits of work and obedience to urban and industrial (as well as military) contexts.

In China, on the other hand, at least at critical moments, peasants chose to resist the imperial authority which they felt to be alien. Even more to the point, they also often struggled to escape the clutches of local loan sharks and other representatives of the commercial exchange system that held the country together economically but did so at the cost of making many peasants feel that they were being systematically cheated. Behind this perception of injustice may lurk a disproportion between growth of wealth and of numbers. Increases in productivity, of a kind that undoubtedly did occur in Japan, presumably came more slowly in China, with the result that as population grew, more and more people had to divide up a total output that was not growing fast enough to maintain existing standards of living.

Under such circumstances, one family's gain was, or at least seemed to be, another's loss. Consequently, instead of holding together on a village basis and then coalescing into a newly self-conscious nation, as the Japanese were able to do, Chinese society fell apart into warring factions. Selfish amoralism flourished as old-fashioned Confucianism went into eclipse. New faiths—the visions of the Taiping leader who claimed to be the younger brother of Jesus Christ, the "Three Principles" proclaimed by Sun Yat-sen, founder of the Kuomintang party, and the Marxism of Mao Tse-tung—struggled to fill the gap without achieving full success.

China is not out of the woods yet; and if the existing political frame holds firm in time to come, China's rulers will be sorely tempted to resort to the politics of military-political expansion, as the Manchus did before them and as united and growing populations have so regularly done elsewhere. The reconquest of Tibet in 1951 showed what a united China could do. Claims derived from the imperial past against the Mongols and Russians in the north and against Vietnam and other southeast Asian lands in the south are readily at hand to justify a policy of renewed expansion, should China's rulers ever decide to act. Surely, an urge to expand will linger just beneath the surface of Chinese politics as long as population pressures remain acute.

But prophecy is not my business, especially when the opaqueness of China's future builds on such obscurities in the past. For even if my suggestions about differences in the rural basis of Chinese and Japanese society are well founded, exactly why Japanese peasants maintained village solidarities and supported national purposes remains as mysterious as why the Chinese did not. Shared values built into Japanese family and village custom required restraint on the part of the superiors and deference on the part of inferiors, but China had a similar heritage that somehow wore thin and then tore to shreds. Why? Did China suffer from rural frag-

41

mentation because of an earlier and more thorough penetration of market relations into agriculture? Or, on the contrary, did governmental intervention inhibit intensified commercial expansion that might have increased productivity and employed surplus rural population? Who knows? But the failure of social cohesion in the countryside seems fundamental and perhaps offers a proximate, powerful, but still only partial explanation for China's modern failures and Japan's successes.[17]

This conclusion suggests a simple—perhaps unduly simplistic—way to understand how some growing populations have descended into intensified rural poverty without engaging in mass political protest. If personal ties and identities are anchored almost wholly within a village community, increasing numbers of the rising generation may simply dictate smaller and smaller parceling of cultivated land and intensified labor on all the bits that remain. As long as physiological survival is possible under these circumstances, rural linkages among neighbors, even when differentiated into owners and tenants, employers and employees, may, perhaps, persist unbroken. Hard times are hard for all, more or less alike. Breaking away from the village community is riskier than staying home, even if that means submitting to impoverishment. Especially when custom dictates a more or less even division of family possessions among all the children, heirs have reason to remain in the village and defend what they have a right to, even if each separate share is too small to sustain the standard of living that the parents had known. Indeed, as long as everyone undergoes approximately the same decline of income, getting poorer may be quite tolerable. Only when some in the village are able to maintain their status or even to increase in wealth while others suffer can community linkages be expected to erode, so that emigration can become attractive enough to counterbalance all the obvious risks, and discontent can start to find violent, political expression.

Is this a plausible portrait of actual rural communities? The case of Java has been much discussed ever since Clifford

Geertz invented the term "agricultural involution" to describe what was happening there.[18] There is no doubt that the rural population of the densely settled rice lands of Java has been getting poorer lately. Java's population seems to have multiplied about ten times since 1800, rising from about 8–10 million to no less than 83 million in 1975.[19] Irrigation was extended to some new areas under the Dutch administration, and plantation production of sugar and other commercial crops employed some of the growing rural population. But their economic survival depended primarily upon expanding the yield of food from intensely cultivated rice paddies. Inequalities of access to land were always present among the villagers, and many families owned no land of their own.

Increasing hardships may have helped to sustain the revolt against the Dutch that made restoration of the pre-World War II colonial regime impossible. With the departure of the Europeans, once independence had been formally achieved in 1949, plantation agriculture decayed rapidly. For a while, the "Green Revolution," by using new, more productive strains of rice seedlings, seemed to promise relief; but disease vulnerability, the high cost of the necessary fertilizer, and continued population growth blunted the success of this technical advance soon after it got under way.[20]

Signs of creeping disaster now abound. The cities depend increasingly on imported rice, for example, while visible signs of malnutrition multiply in the villages.[21] Political disturbances in some of the outer islands of Indonesia have become chronic, partly in reaction against government policies that favor Javanese colonization at the expense of local peoples. But with the exception of a few months in 1965–66, when a military coup d'état was followed by widespread massacre of Communists, Java itself has not seen much sign of political unrest.

How to interpret the situation is problematic. Some observers have emphasized the resilience of village networks of clientage and dependency that share poverty—not equally,

43

but widely—through elaborate exchanges of goods and services. Others emphasize cleavages between rich and poor in Javanese villages and think that political protest was nipped in the bud by the terror of 1965–66, when perhaps as many as 300,000 persons were killed by Moslem bands intent on hunting down Communists.[22] Probably both are true, and other circumstances, for instance, the generally unwarlike traditions of the land, which perhaps make ordinary people less ready to kill one another, must also come into play. Even the warm and equable climate affects behavior because it permits survival on fewer calories than cooler climates require. No one really knows why Java has not suffered internal disorders like those that afflicted China for so long, and it seems useless to speculate.

What the case of Java shows, it seems to me, is that human beings can sometimes acquiesce in impoverishment and continue to multiply, even under extremely precarious conditions of life, without breaking up an inherited framework of village life or resorting to prolonged violence. All the same, it is hard to believe that recent rates of population growth in Java can long persist[23] without precipitating some sort of catastrophe—political, epidemiological, or both at once and mutually reinforcing. But I would have said the same thing thirty years ago and been wrong—proof if any is needed that prophecy is not my business.

Egypt presents a similar conundrum. French experts who accompanied Napoleon to Egypt in 1798 estimated the country's population to be 2.4 million in 1800, whereas the officially tallied total in 1985 was just over twenty times as great, being no less than 48.5 million.[24] Intensified cultivation and technical advances in irrigation permitted notable increases in agricultural production, and efforts at deliberate industrialization and commercial development date back to the time of Muhammad Ali (ruled Egypt 1805–49). But population growth has more than kept up.

Until very recently, and back perhaps into antiquity, the

44

gap between Egyptian villagers and their masters seems to have been greater than was usual elsewhere. Since the first millennium when the Assyrians conquered the country, Egypt has almost always been governed by foreigners of one sort or another. In modern times, Turks and Circassians ruled in a thoroughly feudal fashion until Napoleon's soldiers destroyed their armored cavalry in 1798. Then, in the aftermath of the French invasion, an Albanian adventurer, Muhammad Ali, brought a variegated group of upstarts to power, including some of Napoleon's demobilized French officers.

Muhammad Ali financed his effort at modernization by developing commercial agriculture. The land was thinly occupied at the time, and Muhammad Ali's friends and followers simply seized tracts of fertile soil and then compelled villagers to produce cotton and other cash crops. But the rural population attended to its own subsistence, remaining true to ancient practices, and enjoyed a considerable autonomy as far as their own internal affairs were concerned. Suspicion of outsiders and of the government, whose taxes and conscription for army service bore heavily upon the peasants, was deep-seated and well founded.

All this resembled the situation in Java when Dutch plantation production was in its prime. And as in Java, economic differentiation within village society was the norm. Some owned land, others depended wholly on wages. But such differences were trivial by comparison with the chasm separating the village from outsiders—whether they came in the guise of estate owners, tax collectors, or merely petty traders and moneylenders. Outsiders were exploiters, and village solidarity usually seems to have held firm against them.

When the British brought Egypt under their control after 1882, they did little to change these rural patterns. New irrigation works allowed expansion of the cultivated area, and in some years agricultural output actually managed to grow faster than the population. But this was a fleeting situation.

Traditional poverty remained in the villages, and population growth soon overtook agricultural and industrial-commercial development.

Nationalist sentiment, directed against British and other European intruders, simmered in Egypt's educated urban circles throughout the nineteenth century. It came to a boil following World War II; and after a military coup brought Gamal Abdul Nasser to power in 1952, significant changes came to Egypt's rural society. Yet it was revolution from the top and remained rather superficial. Expropriation of large estates left the same class of small holders in control of village affairs as before. The government's intervention made access to land a little more equitable than before, and absentee land-owners ceased to receive rents; that was all. Landless families did not benefit directly from the reforms, although other measures undertaken by the revolutionary regime did have the effect of opening new opportunities for them in construction work and in new factories.

Simultaneously, the Aswan Dam (built 1960–65) allowed a considerable increase in irrigated area; and new agricultural methods, especially the extensive use of fertilizers and pesticides, began to alter life on the land. For the country as a whole, however, population growth continued to outstrip agricultural productivity, with the result that after about 1970 the urban sector of the population became more and more dependent on foreign grain, supplied mainly from the United States. Parallels with Java's painful situation are therefore obvious.

Javanese expansion, exercised mainly within the Indonesian archipelago, has also been echoed in Egypt. Immediately after he came to power in 1952, Nasser launched an ambitious foreign policy, aimed at extending Egyptian leadership throughout the Arab world and throwing off remnants of colonial dependency. This was entirely in tune with the politics of growing populations and won him enduring popularity, even when initial successes in taking over the Suez Canal in 1956 and forming the United Arab Republic with

46

Syria in 1958 turned into defeat at the hands of the Israelis in 1967.

After Nasser's death in 1970, the Egyptian government adopted a more cautious foreign policy, even making peace with Israel in 1979. Plans for urban and rural development, assisted by substantial American aid and advice, have continued to run a race with ever-rising numbers. In the most recent years, there are even some signs of increased levels of popular consumption, but this was achieved only at the cost of growing indebtedness abroad.

Government policies and repression have so far kept political discontent at bay, though the assassination of President Anwar Sadat by Moslem extremists showed that dissident groups exist. Nonetheless, the population as a whole remains politically inert while enduring hardships that many other peoples would refuse to accept.

What keeps Egypt so quiet? In the villages, remnants of the old community solidarity against outsiders still linger; and as long as village headmen and property owners have a stake in the existing order, they are unlikely to foment any sort of open violence and will discourage others from trying. Moreover, the geography of Egypt makes rural revolt particularly difficult. There is no place to flee from the government's police power. Nonetheless, a vast mass of urban poverty is concentrated in Cairo, where up to eight million people huddle together, and the proportion of urban dwellers in the population as a whole has been rising rapidly in recent decades. Life in the cities, owing to subsidized food prices, is often easier and is always more exciting than rural quiet. Here rather than on the land, future uprisings are likely to occur, if the patience of the population ever gives out.[25]

It is hard to think that peace is not precarious, both in Egypt and in Java. I believe too much in the commonality of human response to think that any part of the world will be permanently exempt from violence when rural populations find that their traditional ways of life have become impossible. The future therefore looks bleak to me, not just in Java

47

and Egypt but in most of the so-called Third World, where vast numbers of peasants and ex-peasants press hard against available resources.

But foresight is weak and prophecy is cheap. Mayhap humankind will muddle through as it has hitherto, less by design than by luck. Our entanglement in ecological processes will certainly set limits to human numbers eventually. Perhaps planned and unplanned demographic adjustments will stumble along, as they have so far, without any really catastrophic disaster and eventually begin to settle toward some new equilibrium between human numbers and the ecosystem that supports us. Time will tell: I assuredly cannot.

3

THE POLITICS OF
DECLINING POPULATIONS

As old age approaches, nearly everyone begins to feel that greater stability in human affairs would be reassuring and restful. Even the young might not mind so very much if the tumults of recent times subsided just a bit. Perhaps that is why demographers and advocates of family planning so often make zero growth population their goal. Assuredly, that looks like a good way to attain greater stability in human affairs, if I am right in suggesting that the global growth of population is the most fundamental and pervasive disturber of human society in modern times, confronting traditional rural communities everywhere, sooner or later, with a brutal impasse of having insufficient land for the rising generation to live on as before.

There are, however, two defects in this vision of what ought to be. First and most obviously, the billions of ex-peasants struggling to achieve full membership in the privileged urban-based exchange systems of our age are unlikely to acquiesce in the disadvantaged, marginal position they occupy. And because they constitute a clear majority of the human race, the rest of us are unlikely to be able to command them to stand still and stop making trouble just for our convenience. Zero growth for population, even if it could be achieved, would only lengthen the fuse on this ticking political time bomb.

Moreover, stable human populations have never existed,

so far as one can tell from the admittedly defective historic record, and are entirely unlikely in time to come. Instead, growth and decay always prevailed. Some populations flourished and expanded at the expense of others that either lost their corporate identities after being engulfed by an expanding neighbor or were biologically extinguished. That is how civilizations spread across the face of the earth—an unmistakable and dominating trend of human history throughout the past five millennia.

Civilizations also depended on an internal circulation of population, bringing surplus youths from the countryside into cities and armies which could not sustain themselves demographically without such rural reinforcement. Other peasants were allowed or compelled to move away from the cities' sometimes overcrowded hinterlands toward frontiers of settlement, whenever fertile fields became available thanks to military and/or epidemiological aggression. Modern times, with which we have been principally concerned, saw these trends accelerate and magnify themselves at first, because improved transport and communications altered the impact of epidemics in civilized societies and exposed isolated peoples to epidemiological destruction more rapidly than before.

Then, beginning about a hundred years ago, and in practice affecting most of the earth only since 1950, this traditional demographic circulation between town and country was profoundly altered when doctors learned how to check the ravages of most infections, so that cities and armies have ceased to be population sinkholes as they used to be. The extraordinary rates of natural increase that now prevail in much of Africa, Latin America, and Asia reflect this combination of circumstances. Consequently, even if birth control were to become universal tomorrow, the dynamics of the present situation assure decades of continued population growth. That is because so many children, already born, will come of age, marry, and beget children of their own in time to come unless something interferes. Only an external catastrophe, arising independently of conscious or unconscious adjustments of birth and death rates, is likely to make much difference in the short run. And, of course, catastrophe is, almost by definition, unlikely to generate a steady state in its wake.

To discredit the notion of steady state still further: even if some populations in some parts of the earth were somehow to succeed in attaining the goal of zero growth, they would do so in a world where other populations were still expanding—or mayhap suffering sudden catastrophic collapse. In such a world, a numerically stable population in one country or region could not expect to isolate itself so as to prevent destabilizing encounters with other parts of the earth where drastic population changes were still in course.

Growing populations do not voluntarily leave their neighbors alone and at ease within existing economic, political, and social frameworks. The history of European and Japanese imperialism in the modern age of population growth surely attests to this propensity; and the long record of civilized expansion into frontier areas in the deeper past tells us the same thing. Indeed, competition for food and other sources of energy and jostling for space in which to grow are characteristic of all forms of life. We cannot hope to escape these ecological realities any more than we can call a halt to history and to biological evolution simply because we are tired of so much change.

Alternating bursts of growth and decay, differing from place to place but trending slowly, very slowly upward, was the way human populations behaved in the deeper past. It is the way other successful plants and animals propagate their kind in the balance of nature. When and if accommodation to the demographic explosion of modern times is attained, one might therefore expect a regimen of modest ups and downs to assert itself again, though a big disturbance to ecological relationships like the modern growth of human populations is liable to trigger a correspondingly big collapse and may require a long time to settle toward minor fluctuations around some future equilibrium.

What will happen is therefore opaque, even for demographers, and it is doubly so for anyone interested in the social and political implications of a demographic regime different from what has prevailed since 1750. One can, of course, look to the past to see what can be learned about human reactions to declining population. Examples are not far to seek, despite the fact that defeated and decaying populations do not usually write history or leave impressive public records behind them.

As we have seen, innumerable isolated peoples were decimated and even entirely destroyed in modern times as a consequence of contacts with infections carried by disease-experienced strangers. The prevailing response to such disaster was to try to escape the scourge of disease by getting on the right side of the supernatural power that seemed clearly to be responsible for unleashing such new and unprecedented epidemics. For peoples so suddenly and severely afflicted, their familiar deities and tutelary spirits were obviously useless. Instead it was the God who keep the strangers from harm who had to be reckoned with, appeased, and obeyed. The success of Christian and Islamic missionaries among previously isolated populations in the Americas, Pacific islands, and some parts of Africa clearly reflected this sort of reasoning among their converts.

Political and cultural implications were considerable. Established elites and religious leaders were discredited by their inability to cope with lethal disease; and even if acceptance of the foreign faith did not halt epidemics (as, of course, it did not), the bewildered and often demoralized remnant found it hard to regain cultural or political autonomy.

Yet efforts to do so abounded and characteristically took the form of millenarian movements, combining motifs from Christian teaching with a vision of the restoration of a purified ancestral way of life from which the intrusive strangers would be entirely excluded. The ghost dance, which spread like wildfire among Plains Indians of the United States in 1889–90, conformed to this pattern, and so did the cargo cults of Oceania. Many other parallel "crisis cults" arose in modern times among peoples who found themselves dying out in ways that seemed both unjust and mysterious.[1]

Millenarian hope for miraculous restoration of the past easily boiled over into the violence of desperation. This is what happened among the Sioux, whose reception of the ghost dance religion was swiftly followed by a final armed encounter with the United States Army in the battle of Wounded Knee, even though the teachings of Wovoka, the prophet who proclaimed the ghost dance, were thoroughly pacific. Sometimes, suicidal behavior became explicit, as when a prophetess persuaded the Xhosa of South Africa in 1856 that if they slaughtered their cattle and destroyed their seed corn, the whites would disappear and a new and better world come miraculously into being. As a result, thousands starved, and resistance to further white aggression became even more hopeless than before.[2]

Such desperate and unavailing efforts to restore a lost world deserve to be counted among the costs of civilized expansion; but, of course, they affected only a few.[3] Population decay among civilized and far more massive populations might be expected to leave greater marks upon the historic record, and in fact that is almost certainly the case. But population statistics for ancient times are so imprecise that definite assertions become highly speculative about, e.g., the fate of the Sumerians in the third millenium B.C. when their language disappeared from everyday speech in Mesopotamia, or of the Mongols in the fourteenth century A.D., whose empire broke up into disparate fragments after the ravages of the plague. In modern times declining civilized populations are rather hard to find, for reasons we have already explored. Nevertheless, I am aware of two cases that are worth thinking about—the Turks of the European provinces of the Ottoman Empire and the Irish after 1845.

Let me begin with the Turks. From the beginning of the Ottoman regime, the Turkish population of the Balkan peninsula probably required continual recruitment to maintain its numbers. The Turks were soldiers and landholders, to begin with. Annual campaigning wasted lives; and urban living, which most Turkish landholders preferred to living out in the villages, did the same. Turkish reinforcements came from central Asia for a while; but conversion of upwardly mobile individuals from among the Christian subject populations was probably more important for maintaining Turkish numbers, though, of course, no one knows the actual volume of either stream of recruits.

After the fourteenth century the flow of Turks from the steppelands dwindled owing to the demographic disaster that the propagation of bubonic plague among the burrowing rodents of the steppe brought in its train. After the seventeenth century, the flow of recruits from the Christian subject populations of the Balkans also dwindled, due to two changes in Ottoman institutions. One was the abandonment of the *devshirme,* whereby the Ottomans had recruited soldiers for the Janissary corps and administrators for the empire by enslaving young men from the Christian population of remote Balkan villages. The other was the deal made, tacitly rather than explicitly, with the Greek elite of Constantinople whereby various high administrative roles in Ottoman society were opened to individuals who remained Christian.

The *devshirme* was abolished in 1638; the opening of new careers to Greeks of the Phanar (a district in Constantinople where the Orthodox patriarch resided) hinged upon the appointment of a Christian as dragoman of the Sublime Porte (i.e., a sort of minister for foreign affairs) in 1669. Thereafter, ambitious and upwardly mobile persons had no need to convert to Islam. It was enough to be or become Greek. As a result, the Greek nationality and identity began to attract persons of Slavic, Romanian, and Albanian background across the breadth of the Balkan peninsula wherever entry into privileged urban occupations came to be reserved, in practice, for persons of Greek language and culture and of the Orthodox faith. Because careers as doctors,[4] merchants, tax farmers, ecclesiastical administrators, and officials in several branches of the Ottoman government were opened to them, conversion to Islam became entirely superfluous. Consequently, recruitment into Turkish ranks dwindled in proportion as that into Greek ranks swelled, and in time the demographic basis for continued Ottoman sovereignty in the Balkans began to wear thin.[5]

To be sure, there were islands of Moslem rural population in the Balkans that shared in the general population surge of the eighteenth and nineteenth centuries. But Moslems of Albanian and Slavic speech began to pull away from identification with the ruling urban Turkish stratum in the course of the nineteenth century, imitating their Christian neighbors by cultivating nationalisms of their own. The handful of rural Turks who remained were outnumbered and eventually overwhelmed by growing Christian populations whose revolts against Ottoman sovereignty, starting in the 1770s, led eventually to imperial collapse.

Turkish response to this situation was largely governed by their military collisions with the European powers. Defeat in war eventually transformed the Ottoman Empire from a restlessly aggressive polity, as it had been from the fourteenth to the sixteenth centuries, into a desperate defender of vanishing greatness in the seventeenth. Indeed, the excited religious sectarianism that Ottoman rulers fell back upon in 1656, when they unleased mystical dervish piety anew in the streets of Constantinople, may be compared to the way the Indian prophet Wovoka, whose mystical experience was subsequently embodied in the ghost dance, sought to defend his people's autonomy.

Both engaged in public rituals inducing mystic ecstasy and generating a warm confidence that supernatural aid would come when needed most. On the other hand, the dervishes did not have to invent new rites or borrow doctrines from the foe, as Wovoka did, but instead could draw on practices and traditions which had been incorporated into Islam centuries before. Moreover, dervish-led revivalism worked in the sense that it allowed the Ottoman government to mobilize a greater effort from the population than before, and even to achieve a modest victory over the Venetians in 1669.[6] But in the longer run the effort to remain true to the Moslem past postponed efforts to match European states on their own terms by military modernization. As a result, the Turks failed to keep up with the great powers of Christian Europe, whereas a generation later under Peter the Great the Russians succeeded in modernizing their military establishment along west European lines but did so only at the cost of religious schism that alienated the Russian peasantry from the state and its agents far more deeply than ever before.

Subsequently, Turkish officials did engage in halfhearted efforts to borrow European military and administrative methods. Wily exploitation of rivalries among the powers of Europe was another device of equal or greater importance for the longevity of the empire. But in the end, demographic pressures from the Christian population, reinforced by the propagation of nationalist ideals among them and supported by the sympathy of western powers for their coreligionists, proved too much. Accordingly, national states supplanted the Ottoman Empire in the Balkans after 1912, while Ottoman rule in Asia ended between 1914 and 1923 with the break-away of the Arab provinces during World War I and the emergence of a Turkish national state based on a demographically buoyant Anatolian peasantry. After systematic exchanges of population had been completed in 1926, only a few scattered remnants of the Turkish population in the Balkans survived outside the boundaries of the new Turkish republic.

The long decline of Turkish numbers and power, relative to competing ethnic and cultural groups in the Balkans, has definitely reversed itself since World War II, for the population of Turkey is now growing far more rapidly than any Balkan people. But that is another story, to which we will return in connection with consideration of recent demographic changes in Germany.

The Turkish experience in the Balkans was probably

quite normal, in the sense that before modern medicine checked the ravages of infectious disease, ruling elites, exposed as they were to the twin risks of frequent campaigning and urban living, had to be recruited from below to sustain their numbers, and whenever recruitment was somehow checked, demographic decay was bound to ensue.

Presumably, a politically dominant population will attempt to hold fast to its privileges when numbers start to shrink just as naturally as a growing population looks for new lands to conquer and new occupational niches to occupy. Expansion, as we saw in chapter 2, is neither easy nor automatic. Holding fast when population decays is probably impossible, at least in a world where other, growingly numerous peoples are increasing their pressure on existing territorial boundaries and politically privileged careers.

It is likely, for instance, that the ruling elements of other polyethnic empires in modern times were also weakened by relative or absolute demographic decay. The Manchus in China and the Moslem military classes that ruled the Mogul empire in India probably did not reproduce themselves as fast as their subjects began to do in the eighteenth and nineteenth centuries; but I am not aware of scholarly discussion of the question, nor, for that matter, have students of Ottoman history inquired very carefully into the demographic background of the political upheavals of the last two centuries. My remarks are therefore speculative rather than grounded in firm fact, but I have little doubt that the scenario I have sketched was operative in the Balkans.[7]

If we turn to Ireland, an utterly different situation confronts us. Population in Ireland began to grow rapidly after about 1770. Price changes in Great Britain induced commercially minded landlords to start raising grain on land that had formerly been left in pasture. This opened jobs for the poor Irish, who used their wages to rent an acre or two on which to plant potatoes. The result was to multiply tiny holdings on each of which a numerous progeny could secure enough to eat, even if they lived in an otherwise desperate poverty. After

57

the end of the Napoleonic Wars in 1815, grain prices fell and the profits of tillage in Ireland shrank. Fields therefore reverted to pasture, and the landlords no longer needed nearly so much agricultural labor. Accordingly, they became reluctant to rent out the bits of lands that the Irish needed for their subsistence.

By 1830 friction between landlords and poor tenants had become acute. Economic hardship slowed but did not check population growth until blight struck the potato fields in 1845 and again in 1846. Enormous numbers died of famine and typhus before effective public relief could be organized, and those who could afford it rushed to emigrate. As a result Ireland's enumerated population of 8.19 million in 1841 (which may have crested at close to 8.5 million in 1845) shrank to 6.55 million in the census of 1851.

Irish population continued to decrease thereafter, bottoming out in the 1960s when only slightly more than half as many people lived on the island as had lived there 120 years previously. Yet during those twelve decades of decline, an aggressively self-assertive Irish nation attained full consciousness and conducted an ultimately successful offensive against the Anglo-Irish landlords and the rest of the Protestant establishment that had fastened its power on the island after the Catholic defeat at the battle of the Boyne in 1689.

In Ireland, therefore, declining numbers did not mean lessened political or economic power. Quite the contrary. Fewer and fewer Irishmen lived better and better as the decades passed, and the rural population began to regulate their numbers by postponing marriage until such time as enough land became available to support each new family. To protect family living standards, only one son could inherit land, and he had to wait until the parental generation was ready to hand over its rights and property. This often meant that the designated heir had to wait until his late thirties or early forties before he could set up a household of his own. Meanwhile, other offspring had to find a career elsewhere, and they commonly headed overseas, either to Great Britain or to

America, where large Irish immigrant communities already existed.[8]

Few rural populations have ever resorted to what Malthus called "prudential restraint" so fiercely or so completely as the Irish did after the famine.[9] The achievement was closely linked with acceptance of new religious and political norms. Thus, in the generation after the famine, a devotional revolution quite transformed the practice of Catholicism in Ireland.[10] The style of Catholic piety that took root in Ireland was pervaded by emphasis upon sexual repression and the sacredness of marriage. It thus reflected and powerfully reinforced the unusual family system that required the young to marry so very late.

In politics, the intensity of the drive for Irish independence drew part of its energy from the more-than-Puritanical repression that Irish piety and family practices imposed upon young men and women. That was because the precautions Irish peasants took to prevent themselves from sinking into abject prefamine poverty delayed, when it did not deny, satisfactory careers for innumerable young men. This assimilated their position to that of Balkan and east European peasant youths, whose inability to live as their parents had done constituted an important background leitmotif of World War I. The fact that in Ireland the rural population was decreasing in numbers while raising its living standard therefore did not bring universal satisfaction in its train. Instead, widespread frustration among the young sustained political effervescence that was only a shade less violent than that which prevailed simultaneously in eastern Europe.

This convergence draws attention to the fact that it is really a mistake to claim that what happened in Ireland after 1845 is an instance of declining population. Globally, Irish population continued to grow, and in Ireland itself natural increase remained very high despite late marriages. Indeed, according to the latest available United Nations figures, Ireland's rate of natural increase in 1985 was greater than that of any other European country, being more than twice that of France, six times that of Great Britain, and infinitely greater than Germany's negative reproduction rate.[11]

In effect, then, the population of Ireland continued to grow after the disastrous setback of 1845–46 but did so by diffusing itself around much of the earth, thinning by half at the center while raising the standard of living in Ireland itself by rigorously tying marriage to possession of land. Such a record constitutes a remarkably successful response to an unusually sharp demographic crisis, and to view Irish demography since 1845 as a case of population decline simply mistakes a part for the whole.

The same may not be said of the population decay that has recently appeared in the census statistics of certain European countries. Germany, Denmark, Hungary, and Austria all had negative rates of natural increase in 1985 according to most recent available statistical summary from the United Nations; and if national statistics did not disguise differential birthrates among diverse ethnic groups in other wealthy, industrialized, and urbanized countries, declining populations in Russia, the United States, France, Great Britain, and even Japan would also become evident, either as actualities of the present and recent past or as demographic certainties (or next thing to it) for the near future.

Differential birthrates among rich and poor have been apparent ever since modern statistics started to be collected; and in a sense, all that is happening in the last decades of the twentieth century is that this pattern has begun to reach across ethnic and cultural boundaries. As a whole nation becomes rich and urbanized, reproduction dwindles. Replacement then must come by recruitment from afar, not from the countryside nearby, as aforetime, and from a rural population that already shares most of the cultural characteristics of the dominant group. Turks in Germany, Algerians in France, Pakistanis and other "New Commonwealth" immigrants in Great Britain, and central Asian Moslems in the Soviet Union all constitute culturally indigestible recruits to the work forces of these countries. Their importance is already considerable, and if prevailing demographic trends continue, their share in the total population of these lands will increase in time to come simply because they reproduce themselves at a higher rate than the dominant ethnic groups, which are, in fact, failing to maintain themselves. In the United States, Mexican, Central American, and Caribbean immigrants, mostly Spanish speaking, play a parallel role, though the fact that they are not marked off from the dominant population by an alien religion makes assimilation into a common body politic perhaps a bit easier than in the European case.

Official statistics often glide over the ethnic shifts that are in train among the rich countries of the earth, and for those countries where statistics do not discriminate between ethnic groups, it is hard to find accurate figures. In Germany, however, Turks and other aliens entered the country as so-called *Gastarbeiter* on the assumption that they would go back home when their work contracts expired. *Gastarbeiter* are therefore not counted a part of the German population even though many families have now lived in Germany for more than two decades and are unlikely to return to their birthplaces willingly.

As a result, changing ethnic balances in Germany are quite clear. German population started to decrease in 1973; simultaneously population counted as foreign increased from 2.98 million in 1970 to 4.36 million in 1985, of which 32.7 percent was Turkish. German birthrates are far below replacement level; Turkish birthrates are far above, and children of Turkish parents, born in Germany, have the right to stay. If vital rates were to remain as they are, Germany would therefore eventually become predominantly Turkish, for the other immigrants (mainly Yugoslavs, Italians, and Greeks) have a birthrate close to or below replacement rates.[12]

To be sure, such an outcome is a very unlikely prospect. Demographic behavior is changeable, and Turkish immigrants living in German cities and working in German factories will not beget so many children when they cease to be youthful newcomers from rural Anatolia. But even if Turkish birthrates in Germany diminish in time to come, the current situation still presents the Germans with an awkward choice between trying to achieve effective assimilation through improved schooling and other civic initiatives or else inducing or compelling the Turks to go back home according to the original *Gastarbeiter* scheme in order to bring other newcomers in to do the nastier jobs which Germans are now unwilling to undertake. If existing ethnic relationships are simply allowed to drift, a two-tiered caste society would arise on German soil, with Germans occupying the managerial and privileged positions, whereas Turks and other aliens would do all the dirty work without enjoying full civic rights.

Very similar patterns exist also in France where, however, the children of Algerians and others of foreign descent born in France are counted as French and have all the legal rights of French citizens. One result is that French statistics make it more difficult to distinguish what is happening demographically as between French residents and citizens with a North African Moslem heritage and other sorts of Frenchmen.[13] According to the census of 1982 there were about 1.4 million Moslems from North Africa in France, and demographers believe that a good many others escaped official enumeration. No one doubts that Moslem numbers are growing rapidly, both by immigration and by natural increase, or that they constitute a minority whose members are almost as sharply segregated from the rest of French society as the Turkish *Gastarbeiter* are from their German self-styled hosts.[14]

Great Britain's census returns show more clearly what has been happening there in recent years. Total population has been almost steady since 1973, with some years of growth and some of decrease; but what forestalls a record of absolute decline, like that of Germany, is the flow of immigrants from what is known as the "New Commonwealth." These newcomers are distinguished from the rest of the population by the color of their skins and by a variety of cultural differences as well. Not all of them occupy menial posts, but most do. In 1981 their total number amounted to about 2.2 million, or 4 percent of the British population as a whole. Ten years earlier they numbered only 1.4 million, or 2.5 percent of the entire population. It is entirely their increase that kept the population total from shrinking.[15]

In the Soviet Union, statistics available to me show a rate of growth slightly greater than that for the United States.[16] But such overall figures, even if accurate, obscure differences between the fertility of central Asian Moslems and those of the European populations of the Soviet Union, whose demography in fact conforms very closely to that of west Europeans. It follows that ethnically Russian populations are on the verge of failing to reproduce themselves or have perhaps already passed that point.[17] Estonians are even further along the slippery slope of demographic decay; but the political effect, so far, has been to enhance Estonian national consciousness. Efforts to protect their ethnic identity by erecting legal consciousness. Efforts to protect their ethnic identity by erecting legal barriers against the Russians recently provoked public demonstrations. The surprising boldness of such action presumably indicates the strength of feeling generated by their fear of ethnic dilution and eventual dissolution.

Unites States statistics also make it difficult to figure out what is happening as between different ethnic groups who share the label "White" in official returns. Immigration, legal and illegal, has been substantial; and barriers to assimilation between newcomers and established elements in the American citizenry are perhaps smaller than in the countries of western Europe where polyethnicity is a new and, for many, an unwelcome situation. But there is no doubt that the portion of the United States citizenry that is of European descent is failing to reproduce itself; and if demographic rates remain unchanged, Hispanics will eventually become numerically predominant.

I should hasten to point out that demographic rates prevailing today will certainly not continue unchanged into the future, though no one can say for sure which way changes will go. Once before, in the depression years of the 1930s, both British and American birthrates dipped below the replacement level; and I am old enough to remember predictions by demographers about how our national population would begin to decline at just about the point in time when in fact the postwar baby boom got under way, thereby utterly confounding the prophets. Similarly sudden shifts of demographic behavior among the privileged may occur in the future, and probably will, though as populations age, fewer remain in the reproductive age bracket. This means that change would have to be very sharp indeed to reverse the downward trend of total numbers in a country like Germany.

Changes at the bottom of the social hierarchy are even more likely. Poor immigrant populations may not long persist in begetting large families. All depends on whether they accept the prevailing ideals and family mores of the dominant groups and begin to seek (and attain) a higher standard of living for themselves, or whether they hold fast to their own customs and patterns of demographic behavior and become a self-perpetuating underclass.

There are obvious difficulties besetting either of these paths toward the future. Assimilation involves betrayal of old values and ways of life. Second-generation immigrants, embarked on this course, may find their way blocked by the unwillingness of older elements in the population to accept them as equals and fellow citizens. Such experiences are liable to generate a culture of defiance among the young, who may find themselves alienated from their parents and from the land of their parents' origin, as well as from the host country in which they find themselves. Signs of defiant, often self-destructive, behavior abound in Europe[18] as well as in the United States and lie behind at least part of the drug epidemic that afflicts our cities. Costs for all concerned, and especially for those who find themselves caught between two worlds and belonging to neither, are very great.

On the other hand, remaining loyal to ancestral ways in

64

a new environment creates a caste system reserving different occupations for particular ethnic groups. Urban societies constructed on this principle are in fact very old. Indeed, one may argue that polyethnicity organized on caste lines is the characteristic norm of civilized urban society, reflecting the necessity, under traditional, premodern demographic conditions, of replenishing city populations by welcoming recruits from distant and alien lands—or taking them as slaves when voluntary immigration fell short.

From this perspective, the expectation that immigrants would and should assimilate to a dominant culture became more or less of a reality in the recent past only because general population growth supplied an ample number of recruits for cities from within the radius of a few score of miles. Because such immigrants already shared most of the cultural characteristics of the established urban classes to which they were then expected to assimilate their ways, legal equality and a career open to talent regardless of origins became an attractive and plausible ideal. It was more or less realized in practice in western European lands from the eighteenth century or before, but in eastern Europe the ideal of ethnic uniformity cost much bloodshed and political violence before it was achieved (more or less) in the wake of World Wars I and II.

The troubled ethnic history of eastern Europe should be of special interest to Americans because our polyethnicity partially recapitulated the historic experience of eastern Europe. Urban ethnic pluralism in eastern Europe dated back to the later Middle Ages, when that part of the Continent was a rapidly developing frontier land. Accordingly, rulers of Poland, Transylvania, and other states extended special privileges to Jews and to German merchants and artisans in order to accelerate urban development and thereby improve state revenues. (The Turks, a little later, were hospitable to Jews, Armenians, and Greeks for similar reasons; the Russians lagged a little behind, allowing enclaves of foreign merchants and professionals to arise in their cities after about 1600.)

This official strategy of encouraging deliberate urban development had the unforeseen result of establishing enduring urban castes that were insulated by religious and cultural differences from the environing population. Some of them still survive.

In modern times, the frontier role played by the United States and other countries of European settlement overseas also established ethnically diverse populations. They, too, were organized along caste lines, publicly embedded not so much in religion (though that mattered, too, when Irish immigration first flooded into Protestant New England) as in differences of skin color. For a long time, American ideals of freedom and equality did not extend to blacks and Indians; and despite repeated legal enactments since 1863, the gap has never been fully bridged. Our cities have indeed been melting pots for many European immigrants; but whether they will be for Mexican, Caribbean, and Central American newcomers remains to be seen, just as it remains to be seen how ethnic relationships will develop in Europe when recruits to their cities come not from a culturally contiguous hinterland but from Moslem and other sharply contrasting cultural backgrounds.

Politically speaking, one must expect considerable volatility in public responses to what is still a new and perhaps unstable demographic regime in the rich, urbanized countries of the earth. Getting used to having foreigners around may be harder for Europeans and Japanese than for Americans and other inhabitants of the erstwhile frontier lands where ethnic mingling has existed for generations. Interestingly enough, the cessation of population growth in the industrialized heartlands of the European continent coincides with changes in EEC regulations which aim at eliminating legal barriers to migration among the European nations themselves. It is conceivable that in time to come people within the EEC will begin to identify themselves less as members of a particular nation than as Europeans. That, of course, would significantly alter the boundary between "us" and "them," but it would still exclude Moslem and other strangers who are already on the ground, increasing in number and themselves in a very unstable state, both culturally and demographically. The one thing that seems certain is that the difference between European and American society will diminish as both become more obviously polyethnic than in times past.

Shrinking populations are not likely to sustain expansion abroad. Keeping what one has already is a more appropriate preoccupation for governments presiding over an ethnic mix in which the dominating element of the population is diminishing in number. But offense may sometimes be the best defense. I referred a moment ago to recent Estonian efforts at aggressively defending themselves. The parallel behavior of French Canadians is rather better known. Before World War II, rural *habitants* were prolific enough to maintain the French proportion of the population of Canada at about 30 percent, even though most immigrants chose to assimilate to the English-speaking style of Canadianism. Some even looked ahead to an ultimate victory of the cradle that might someday restore French preponderance in the whole country or at least in several provinces beyond the stronghold of Quebec itself. But the cultural integument that had sustained large families among the French since colonial times collapsed rather abruptly during and after World War II, when young people decided to disregard the teachings of the Catholic church about birth control. Accordingly, in the 1960s French Canadian birthrates sank below those of English-speaking Canadians and fell far short of replacement rates.[19]

All of a sudden, the French position in the country seemed endangered. The response was an exacerbated French nationalism, seeking either to withdraw from the Canadian confederation entirely or, at a minimum, to safeguard French language and culture by legal proscription of the use of English in many accustomed situations in the province of Quebec. This and the parallel Estonian example show that acquiescence in loss of status in face of diminishing numbers ought not to be taken for granted, even among a people that had formerly been a rather quiet minority.

The tendency toward aggressive self-assertion in face of diminishing numbers may also be recognized in nativist rhetoric directed against Algerians in France, Turks in Germany, and West Indians and Pakistanis in Britain. So far, such themes have remained on the fringes of national politics in each of these countries. Memory of Nazi crimes and the continuing momentum of European integration pull in an opposite direction, just as the United States' tradition of civil rights and opportunity for all has damped back attacks on blacks and Hispanics. But no one can be sure that some surge of anger may not break through such barriers in time to come, especially if the dominant ethnic groups of each country begin to feel really threatened.

Ethnic frictions and rivalries are far nearer the surface in the Soviet Union. Efforts by Great Russians to sustain their hegemony in the absence of the abundant flow of peasant manpower that supplied the needs of the state from the time of Ivan the Terrible to that of Stalin face obstacles that make the situation of Germans in Germany look positively comfortable. Bruises arising from Russian aggressions of the past remain fresh in the recollection of Ukrainians and other European nationalities of the Soviet Union; while in central Asia large Turkish and Iranian populations remain socially and culturally distinct and at least vaguely Moslem, despite decades of ideological blandishment by atheistic Communist propaganda and considerable technical change in both urban and rural life.

Reflecting upon the demographic changes that seem to be in train in the world, I am tempted to recognize some deep-seated natural rhythm whereby a growing population, after two hundred years (say, six to eight generations) of successful expansion at the expense of rivals, ceases to reproduce itself and so in turn gives way to others. In ancient Greece and Rome, as I suggested in chapter 1, it was perhaps the disruptive effect of military service and urban living on rural family patterns that halted population growth and invited the wholesale resort to slavery that Marx took as the characteristic form of labor relations in the ancient world.

In modern times, medical science made urban living safe from ordinary lethal infections, and even armies became immune from all but wounds, which in former times were a comparatively minor cause of campaign deaths. Yet, urbanism remains inimical to child bearing and rearing in a way that rural living is not, and with modern methods of birth control young women are able to regulate births to suit themselves. Most city dwellers prefer a style of life that is incompatible with what St. Augustine once described as the "incessant squalor of babes." Having given birth to one or two demanding infants, they want no more, even though for statistical reasons an average of a little more than two children per woman of breeding age is needed to replace each generation as it ages and dies.

Thus it may be true that even though the triumphs of modern medicine eliminated infections as a major factor in urban die-off, the success with which other medical researchers discovered easy and effective methods of birth control may restore the age-old pattern of demographic circulation between town and country, rich and poor, upon which civilized society has depended ever since the third millennium B.C.

Globally, there remain billions of peasants and ex-peasants who are ready and eager to move into places vacated by wealthier, urbanized populations. Supply indeed far exceeds demand for labor, even of the humblest sort. One can therefore recognize that the traditional circulation of populations remains very much in working order, with the difference that now, as in the early phases of civilized history, it has become necessary to cross cultural demarcation lines to find recruits for the most powerful and richest cities of the earth.

Let me close with a biblical text. "Blessed are the meek," said Jesus, "for they shall inherit the earth."[20] He uttered

these words in an overcrowded Roman province where rebellion simmered among a rural population that could not
find enough land to live on in traditional ways. In the course
of the next century, the Jews of Palestine did not remain
meek. Instead, repeated risings and Roman repression almost
emptied the lands of its Jewish inhabitants. Those who lis-
tened to the Sermon on the Mount therefore did not themselves inherit very much of the earth. But in the longer run,
the saying was and still is perfectly true, with this additional
gloss: those who succeed in inheriting the earth cease to be
meek and thereby open a path for successors to come behind
them and sustain the circulation between wealthy town and
poverty-stricken countryside that has maintained human society since cities first appeared.

The really surprising thing is that this ancient pattern
still looks as though it might maintain itself in spite of all our
clever interventions in natural ecological processes. But all
the cleverness in the world cannot emancipate us from the
balances of nature. This enduring pattern of human demography—if it does endure, for in closing I must stress how
faulty demographic prophecy remains despite all the numer-
ical sophistication of the experts—ought to remind us of
those limits.

That, indeed, has been my central purpose here. I have
emphasized the role of demography in human affairs and
tried to show how politics rides on currents of biological ebb
and flow. Only by recognizing these levels of human life and
the constraints and possibilities they offer to conscious and
deliberate management can we expect to become more nearly
able to navigate successfully amidst the tumult of our times.

Such thinking will not eliminate the fallibility of foresight. Fallibility remains essential to the human condition.
One cannot really wish for its elimination from our lives. Yet
as more or less rational persons we also wish to extend the
domain of understanding and deliberate control. Poised between these antimonies, human beings remain unique in the
balance of nature, because we use words and ideas to orga-

nize our behavior and to change it. Thus, awareness of demographic trends we dislike may permit us to change them.

Assuredly, demography has affected behavior—always. Even a partial understanding of that dimension of the past ought to increase the precision and grace with which we respond to ebbs and flows of the future. And that is why population and politics are worth thinking about.

NOTES

I
---

1. Michael W. Flinn, *The European Demographic System, 1500–1820* (Baltimore, 1981), p. 76 and passim; Ping-ti Ho, *Studies in the Population of China, 1368–1953* (Cambridge, Mass., 1959), p. 278; Robert W. Fogel and Stanley Engerman, *Time on the Cross: The Economics of American Negro Slavery* (Boston, 1974), pp. 24–29; Nicholas Sanchez-Albornoz, *The Population of Latin America: A History* (Berkeley and Los Angeles, 1974), pp. 86–145; Russell Thornton, *American Indian Holocaust and Survival: A Population History since 1492* (Norman, Okla., 1987); Marcel Reinhard and André Armengaud, *Histoire générale de la population mondiale* (Paris, 1961), pp. 202ff.

2. Cf. R. L. Carneiro and D. F. Hilse, "On Determining the Probable Rate of Population Growth during the Neolithic," *American Anthropologist* 68 (1966): 177–81; Mark N. Cohen, *The Food Crisis in Prehistory: Overpopulation and the Origins of Agriculture* (New Haven, 1977).

3. After making this suggestion in William H. McNeill, *Plagues and Peoples* (New York, 1976), pp. 196ff., I was surprised to find that such a distinguished demographic historian as R. S. Schofield rejected it out of hand. But other explanations of the modern upsurge of human numbers are not adequately global. Changes in marriage patterns, food intake, and cleanliness, to cite the factors English demographers have recently preferred, cannot plausibly be extended to China or the rest of the world where similar growth appeared between 1750 and 1850. Cf. E. A. Wrigley and R. S. Schofield, *The Population History of England, 1541–1871,* (Cambridge, Mass., 1981); Thomas McKeown, *The Modern Rise of Population,* (London, 1976); James C. Ridley, "Insects and European Mortality Decline," *American Historical Review* 91 (1986): 833–58. All agree that the fading away of lethal epidemics was the immediate, obvious change in European demographic experience. The disputed question is why? Cf. D. E. C. Eversley, "Population, Economy, and Society,"

in D. C. Glass and D. E. C. Eversley, *Population in History: Essays in Historical Demography* (London, 1965), p. 57.

4. Cf. William H. McNeill, "The Eccentricity of Wheels, or Eurasian Transportation in Historical Perspective," *American Historical Review* 92 (1987): 1111–26.

5. For an appreciation of the heroic echo of antiquity a cultivated European found in contemporary Serbia, see Leopold von Ranke, *A History of Servia and the Servian Revolution,* 2d ed. (London, 1848). For the breakup of old forms of self-help, see Jozo Tomasevich, *Peasants, Politics, and Economic Change in Yugoslavia* (Stanford, Calif., 1955), pp. 178ff.

6. Olwen H. Hufton, *The Poor in Eighteenth Century France, 1750–1789* (Oxford, 1974) offers a magistral account of resultant conditions.

7. Cf. G. H. Slicher van Bath, *The Agrarian History of Western Europe, A.D. 500–1850* (New York, 1963), pp. 221ff.

8. Arthur Young, *Travels in France during the Years 1787, 1788, and 1789* (rept. New York, 1969).

9. The fallow in traditional grain husbandry served the function of clearing the field of weeds. By plowing the fallow during the growing season, weed seeding cycles were interrupted, with the result that grain planted in the following year could escape heavy competition from weeds. Anthropomorphic thinking equated fallowing with resting the soil, but the geologic processes that might restore fertility to exhausted fields are far too slow to make any perceptible difference in a single year. Hoe cultivation of the new crops also killed weeds and so served the same purpose as fallowing had done, thus producing a new and valuable crop without diminishing grain yields at all.

10. Ester Boserup, *The Conditions of Agricultural Growth: The Economics of Agrarian Change under Population Pressure* (London, 1965) uses European and Asian examples to argue that intensified land use is a general and predictable response to population growth. Like many economists, she pays little attention to cultural and social resistances to market incentives of the sort that prevented the peasant proprietors from responding as flexibly as landlords did to the new possibilities of eighteenth-century Europe. In the long run the market may be sovereign and she may be right; but I am more impressed by the exceptional circumstances that allowed European nations to respond as successfully and rapidly as they did to the unprecedented problem of population growth than I am by any sort of predictability, certainty, or even probability.

11. One calculation put as much as a sixth of the Parisian population of 1789 in the class of rootless immigrants who had yet to find a stable job or achieve inscription as legal residents of the city. George Rudé, *Paris and London in the Eighteenth Century: Studies in Popular Protest* (New York, 1971), pp. 35–36.

12. On the decay of crowd action, cf. Georges LeFebvre, *The French Revolution from 1793 to 1799* (London, 1964), pp. 70, 145; Jacques Godechot, *Les Révolutions, 1770–1799* (Paris, 1970), pp. 94–95.

13. Reinhard and Armengaud, pp. 238–68, treat the peculiarities of French demography betwen 1801 and 1914 in some detail. For the suggestion that military experience of sex may have affected French birthrates, see Jacques Dupaquier, "Problèmes démographiques de la France napoléonienne," *Annales historiques de la Révolution française* 42 (1970): 21.

14. The progress of birth control across Europe is elegantly and precisely represented in maps at the back of Ansley J. Coale and Susan C. Watkins, eds., *The Decline of Fertility in Europe* (Princeton, N.J., 1980).

15. Daniel R. Headrick, *The Tools of Empire: Technology and European Imperialism in the Nineteenth Century* (New York, 1981) shows how a remarkable (if transitory) technological superiority made European imperial expansion both cheap and easy.

16. See, for instance, H. J. Habbakuk, *Population Growth and Economic Development since 1750* (New York, 1971), p. 48: "I am not arguing, then, that the effects of population growth were simple or straightforward, or that they were invariably favorable. But I find it difficult to interpret the eighteenth century without supposing that, on balance, population growth was a stimulus to the development of the [British] economy."

17. Rudé, pp. 268–92.

18. Cf. table 7.9 in Wrigley and Schofield, p. 213.

19. On the Continent, dependence on potatoes among the poor was still incipient when the potato blight struck in 1845. This spared the population from the catastrophic famine that hit Ireland, but even so the "hungry forties" were long remembered. On potatoes and population, cf. Redcliffe N. Salaman, *The History and Social Influence of the Potato* (Cambridge, 1949); William L. Langer, "Europe's Initial Population Explosion," *American Historical Review* 69 (1963): 1–17; K. H. Connell, *The Population of Ireland, 1750–1845* (Oxford, 1950), pp. 121–62.

20. David Mitrany, *The Land and the Peasants in Rumania: The War and Agrarian Reform, 1917–21* (New Haven, 1930); Henry Roberts, *Rumania: Political Problems of an Agrarian State* (London, 1951).

21. Cf. E. L. Jones, *The European Miracle* (Cambridge, 1981) for a reflective discussion of Europe's economic advantages, now partly retracted in E. L. Jones, *Growth Recurring* (New York, 1988).

22. Reinhard and Armengaud, p. 307; Donald W. Treadgold, *The Great Siberian Migration* (Princeton, N.J., 1957).

23. Vladimir Dedijer, *The Road to Sarajevo* (London, 1957), pp. 185–97; Woodford D. McClellan, *Svetozar Markovic and the Origins of Balkan Socialism* (Princeton, N.J., 1964); Tomasevich.

_____ 2 _____

1. Eugen Weber, *Peasants into Frenchmen* (Stanford, Calif., 1976) shows how slowly the gap between town and country was closed, even in France. As for Great Britain, rural laborers got the right to vote only in 1884.

2. Sherburne F. Cook and Woodrow Borah, *Essays in Population History: Mexico and the Caribbean,* 2 vols. (Berkeley, Calif., 1971–73) summarizes the pioneering work of these two scholars who first established the magnitude of the Indian die-off. Challenges to their high estimates of pre-Columbian population have been made, but no one now doubts the magnitude of the disaster. For Amerindian population history in the United States and Canada, see Thornton.

3. McNeill, *Plagues and Peoples,* pp. 60–67, explains the process and its climatic limits. In tropical Africa and in less degree also in India and southeast Asia, local populations inured to survival in the presence of tropical diseases could meet the bearers of civilized diseases on more or less even terms, exchanging one set of lethal infections for another. Indeed, the tropical diseases of Africa were so formidable to newcomers that it was they who died, not the natives.

4. Four to five times as many Africans as Europeans crossed the Atlantic before 1800 according to the best available estimates, and of the whites a majority were indentured servants. Compulsory labor thus played a very large role in repopulating the Americas with immigrants from the Old World. Cf. Stanley L. Engerman, "Servants to Slaves to Servants: Contract Labor and European Expansion," in H. van den Boogart and P. C. Emmers, eds., *Colonialism and Migration: Indentured Labor before and after Slavery* (The Hague, 1966).

5. The best account of periodic land redistribution and other traits of the Russian *mir* known to me is from the pen of a nineteenth-century British diplomat and eyewitness, Donald Mackenzie Wallace, *Russia,* 5th ed. (London, 1877).

6. Cf. Geroid T. Robinson, *Rural Russia under the Old Regime* (New York, 1949), pp. 138–207 and passim.

7. Cf. Kenneth F. Kiple, *The Caribbean Slave: A Biological History* (Cambridge, 1984).

8. Color and race consciousness depended more on the sex ratio among the dominant whites than on differences between Catholic and Protestant views of slavery. Where few white women crossed the ocean, as was the case in Brazil and in Spanish colonies, mestizos abounded and race mixture prevailed because only a small aristocratic element had access to white wives. The English, however, sent a sufficient number of white women with the early colonists to allow a replica of European family norms to cross the ocean. Under these circumstances, color consciousness and discrimination became acute simply

because a persistent surplus of males among new arrivals from Europe made the ideal of white marriage as the only acceptable form of sexual union difficult to maintain. The transformation of manners among the British servants of the East India Company after P & O steamships began to carry Englishwomen to India in the 1840s offers rather dramatic support for the thesis that sex balance among immigrants made all the difference—not any specially intense Protestant or north European racism.

9. Dependency theory holds, with considerable plausibility, that the interconnectedness of the world makes it doubly difficult for weaker, dependent economies to duplicate the achievements of the rich, dominant ones. For a magistral presentation of this idea, see Immanuel Wallerstein, *The Modern World System,* 3 vols. (New York, 1974–89). Yet the case of Japan surely shows that dependency is not irreversible.

10. Thomas C. Smith, *The Agrarian Origins of Modern Japan* (Stanford, Calif., 1959) and Francesca Bray, *The Rice Economies: Technology and Development in Asian Societies* (Oxford, 1986) do much to illuminate the peculiarities of rice paddy agriculture.

11. Irene B. Taeuber, *The Population of Japan* (Princeton, N.J., 1958), pp. 29–33; Susan B. Hanley and Kozo Yamamura, *Economic and Demographic Change in Preindustrial Japan* (Princeton, N.J., 1977), p. 233; James Lee, Cameron Campbell, and Guofu Tan, "Price and Population History in Rural Fengtian, 1772–1873," paper delivered at conference on Economic Methods for Chinese Historical Research, Oracle, Ariz., January 1988.

12. Figures for 1985 are from United Nations, *Demographic Yearbook, 1985* (New York, 1987); the eighteenth-century figures come from Dwight H. Perkins, *Agricultural Development in China, 1368–1986* (Chicago, 1969), p. 216, and from Taeuber, p. 22.

13. China possessed the skills and organization required for transoceanic navigation but never chose to compete with the European discovery of America by settling the Pacific coast of the New World. This deliberate abdication, building on the dismantlement of the navy after 1435, certainly changed the balance of the world incalculably. On Chinese naval capabilities, see Joseph Needham, *Science and Civilisation in China,* vol. 4, pt. 3, "Nautics," (Cambridge, 1978).

14. Cf. Elizabeth J. Perry, *Rebels and Revolutionaries in North China, 1845–1945* (Stanford, Calif., 1980); Philip Kuhn, *Rebellion and Its Enemies in Late Imperial China* (Cambridge, Mass., 1970); Benjamin J. Schwartz, *Chinese Communism and the Rise of Mao* (Cambridge, Mass., 1951).

15. Nicholas R. Lardy, *Agriculture in China's Modern Economic Development* (Cambridge, 1983), pp. 149–51, says grain production dropped by 26.4 percent in 1961 and estimates a "net loss of 26 million persons" from famine.

16. Taeuber, p. 201.

17. Mark Elvin, *The Pattern of the Chinese Past* (London, 1973) is perhaps the best-known effort to explain China's modern failure to keep up with the West, but his notion of a "high level equilibrium trap" has not won very much support. My reflections on the importance of rural cohesion for Japan's success and China's failures were stimulated by Thomas C. Havens, *Farm and Nation in Modern Japan: Agrarian Nationalism, 1870–1940* (Princeton, N.J., 1974); Hsiao-Tung Fei, *Peasant Life in China: A Field Study of Country Life in the Yangtse Valley* (London, 1962); Hsiao-Tung Fei, *China's Gentry: Essays in Rural-Urban Relations* (Chicago, 1953); William Parrish and Martin Whyte, *Village and Family in Contemporary China* (Chicago, 1978); Richard Madsen, *Morality and Power in a Chinese Village* (Berkeley, Calif., 1984); and most directly perhaps by James C. Scott, *The Moral Economy of the Peasant: Rebellion and Subsistence in Southeast Asia* (New Haven, 1976).

18. Clifford Geertz, *Agricultural Involution: The Process of Ecological Change in Indonesia* (Berkeley, Calif., 1963).

19. Donald W. Fryer and James C. Jackson, *Indonesia* (London, 1977), p. 142. Java's early population has often been set at only 4.5 million in accord with an estimate made by Stamford Raffles; but he seriously underestimated the facts as they existed in his day according to Bram Peper, "Population Growth in Java in the 19th Century: A New Interpretation," *Population Studies* 24 (1970): 71–83.

20. Cf. Richard W. Franke, "Miracle Seeds and Shattered Dreams in Java," *Natural History* 84 (1974): 11–18, 84–88.

21. Benjamin White, "Population, Involution, and Employment in Rural Java," in Gary E. Hansen, ed., *Agricultural and Rural Development in Indonesia* (Boulder, Colo., 1981), pp. 130–31.

22. James C. Scott, pp. 193ff., explores this question incisively but without reaching a definite conclusion. Cf. Jennifer Alexander and Paul Alexander, "Shared Poverty as Ideology: Agrarian Relationships in Colonial Java," *Man* 17 (1982): 597–619 for emphasis on conflict; Geertz for the opposite view.

23. The populations of Indonesia grew from 133 million in 1976 to 163 million in 1985 according to the United Nations, *Demographic Yearbook, 1985*. More than half of this total is Javanese, but I have not found really recent population estimates for the island proper.

24. Figure for 1800 from Abdel R. Omran, ed., *Egypt: Population Problems and Prospects* (Chapel Hill, N.C., 1973), p.9; for 1985, *United Nations, Demographic Yearbook*, p. 151.

25. Alan Richards, *Egypt's Agricultural Development, 1800–1980: Technical and Social Change* (Boulder, Colo., 1982) gives an instructive account of changes in Egyptian rural life. Tom Little, *Modern Egypt* (London, 1967) and Derek Hopwood, *Egypt: Politics and Society, 1945–1984* (Boston, 1985) are more general accounts that I also found useful.

3

1. Weston LaBarre, "Materials for a History of Studies of Crisis Cults: A Bibliographic Essay," *Current Anthropology* 12 (1971): 3–42 surveys the theme admirably. His category of crisis cults includes examples from groups made desperate not by declining but by rising populations like the Taipings of China. Either circumstance, when accustomed ways of life become impossible, can generate crisis cults. Convergences in ideas and political-military behavior among both sorts of sectarians are very close.

2. Paul Bohannan and Philip Curtin, *Africa and the Africans,* 3d ed. (Prospect Heights, Ill., 1988), pp. 372–73.

3. Millenarianism among peoples made desperate by rising population pressure, on the other hand, has had enormous and enduring consequences, as the history of Judaism between 168 B.C. and A.D. 135 and the history of early Christianity both illustrate.

4. The medical profession had been the avenue whereby Greeks achieved intimate access to the topmost levels of the Ottoman government. It was when the grand vizier asked his personal physician, Panagiotis Nicoussias, to negotiate a peace with Venice in 1669 that a gratified Ottoman government made the doctor-diplomat the first dragoman of the Sublime Porte. Cf. William H. McNeill, *Venice, the Hinge of Europe, 1081–1797* (Chicago, 1974), pp. 213–14.

5. I should point out that no Balkan census for the centuries after 1699 exists, so my remarks about numbers are impressionistic, not statistical. Moreover, new converts rallied to Islam in the seventeenth century in Crete, Albania, and the mountainous region of southern Bulgaria. These humble rural folk retained their local languages, however, remaining separate from the Turks of the empire, just as did the Bosnian Moslems, whose conversion dated back to the fourteenth century. These Moslem groups constituted a reserve of military manpower, well fitted for irreglar war; but living, as they did, mainly as shepherds and mountaineers, they were ill-suited to most urban employments and did not in fact do much to reinforce Turkish numbers in the important centers of the empire.

6. Ayatollah Khomeni did much the same in Iran in 1979, but his sounding board was a pullulating rural and newly urbanized population, not a decaying one as in the Ottoman instance. This looks like another case in which response to opposite demographic emergencies converged. On rural response to Khomeni, see Eric J. Hoogland, *Land and Revolution in Iran, 1960–1980* (Austin, Tex., 1982).

7. Balkan history is so disfigured by modern nationalisms that most historians do not want to admit that persons changed nationalities in times past simply by rising in the social scale and deliberately taking on new ethnic identities. In the nineteenth century such behavior became treason to the nation of one's birth, and conversion to Islam

always carried a taint of treason in the eyes of Christian churchmen. But conversions certainly occurred and constituted an essential basis of Turkish strength in the early days of the empire. See Spyros Vryonis, *The Decline of Medieval Hellenism in Asia Minor and the Process of Islamization from the Eleventh through the Fifteenth Century* (Berkeley, Calif., 1971).

8. Conrad M. Arensberg, *The Irish Countryman: An Anthropological Study* (New York, 1937) describes Irish rural life with admirable sensitivity. The pattern of late marriage and delayed inheritance of rights to the land that he discerned in the 1930s became general after the famine, but signs of its development can be traced in demographic statistics from about 1830. See Connell, pp. 41–51.

9. The closest analogue I am aware of is the way German settlers on the Danubian frontier regulated their numbers and protected their superior status as against surrounding Slavs and Romanians by preserving farm size inviolate. Extra sons emigrated, often moving back to more developed German lands to make a career in town. A favored pattern was to pursue a university education so as to qualify for a post in the Hapsburg bureaucracy. This provided the monarchy with a flow of faithful servants but had the side effect of freezing the development of German settlements in Bachka and Banat at a dispersed rural level, where, as a small privileged class, they were vulnerable to being displaced completely after World Wars I and II. On these German frontier settlements and their ceiling of growth, see William H. McNeill, *Europe's Steppe Frontier* (Chicago, 1964).

10. Cf. Emmett Larkin, "The Devotional Revolution in Ireland, 1850–1875," *American Historical Review* 77 (1972): 625–52.

11. United Nations, *Demographic Yearbook, 1985,* table 4, shows Eire with a rate of natural increase of 9.1 per thousand, Northern Ireland with 7.7, France with 4.0, and Great Britain with 1.5. The German Federal Republic's rate was − 1.9.

12. Jurgen Bahr and Hans Gans, "The Federal Republic of Germany," in Allan Findlay and Paul White, eds., *West European Population Change* (London, 1986), pp. 142–46, 156–61. The situation has provoked considerable debate, as for instance, Lutz Franke and Hans W. Jurgens, eds., *Keine Kinder—Keine Zukunft?* (Boppard-am-Rhein, 1978); Varena McRae, *Die Gastarbeiter: Daten, Fakten, Probleme* (Munich, 1981).

13. The further fact that many French settlers withdrew to France after 1962 when Algeria became independent means that Algerian birth does not always signify Moslem identity.

14. See, for example, André Chazalette and Pierre Michaud, *La Deuxième génération d'immigrants dans la région Rhône Alpes* (Lyons, 1977); Philip Ogden and Hilary Winchester, "France," in Findlay and White, pp. 134–39.

15. Anthony Champion, "Great Britain," in Findlay and White, p. 228.

16. United Nations, *Demographic Yearbook, 1985,* table 4, attributes a

natural rate of increase of 8.8 per thousand to the USSR as against a
rate of 7.0 for the United States.

17. Ansley J. Coale, Barbara Anselm, and Erna Harm, *Human Fertility
in Russia since the Nineteenth Century* (Princeton, N.J., 1979).
18. Stephen Castles et al., *Here for Good: Western Europe's New Ethnic
Minorities* (London, 1984), pp. 159–89.
19. Warren E. Kalbach and Wayne W. McVey, *The Demographic Basis of
Canadian Society,* 2d ed. (Toronto, 1971), p. 99.
20. Matthew 5:5.

INDEX